Island of South Georgia

SOUTHERN OCEAN

54°00'S

35°40'

N

0 5 10 15 20 25 mi

0 5 10 15 20 25 30 35 km

36°40' 36°20' 36°00'W 35°40'

Harbour

Leith Harbour
Cape Saunders
FORTUNA GLACIER
Fortuna Bay
Stromness
Stromness Bay
Husvik
KÖNIG GLACIER
Larsen Point
Jason Harbour
Cumberland Bay
NEUMAYER GLACIER
Cumberland West Bay
Maiviken
Right Whale Rocks
West Skerry
East Skerry
Cobblers Cove
Godthul
Cape George
LARSEN PLATEAU 2856'
Grytviken
Cumberland East Bay
Moraine Fiord
Ocean Harbour

54°20'

Newark Bay
KJERULF GLACIER
Mt. Sugartop 7623'
LYELL GLACIER
HAMBERG GLACIER
HARKER GLACIER
NORDENSKJÖLD GLACIER
Hound Bay
Jacobsen Bight
CHRISTOPHERSEN GLACIER
RANGE
St. Andrews Bay
Hauge Strait
Mt. Paget 9625'
Mt. Roots 7483'
Nordenskjöld 7725'
Mt. Fagan 2967'
Cape Harcourt
Undine South Harbour
BRÖGGER GLACIER
ROSS GLACIER
Royal Bay
Cape Charlotte
ALLARDYCE
Pickersgill Islands
SALVESEN RANGE
Gold Harbour

54°40'

SEA
NOVOSILSKI GLACIER
TWITCHER GLACIER
Mt. Carse 7649'
Iris Bay
Diaz Cove
Wirik Bay
SALOMON GLACIER
Damien Bay
Cooper Bay
Cooper Sound
Drugalski Fjord
Hamilton Bay
Cooper Island
PHILIPPI GLACIER
Larsen Harbour
Cape Disappointment
Smaaland Cove
Esbensen Bay

54°56'

36°40' 36°20' 36°00'W 35°40'

P9-EKX-846

ANTARCTIC

OASIS

ANTARCTIC OASIS

Under the Spell of South Georgia

TEXT AND PHOTOGRAPHS BY

TIM AND PAULINE CARR

W.W. Norton & Company

NEW YORK   LONDON

DEDICATION

To the two yachts and their crews that inspired us to follow in their wakes to South Georgia:

Totorore sailed by Gerry Clark and assisted by Malcolm Roberts, Andreas Von Meyer,
Julia Von Meyer and Chris Sale who counted king penguins and wandering albatrosses
for the British Antarctic Survey against great odds in the winters of 1984 and 1985
and
Damien II with Jérôme and Sally Poncet and their sons Dion, Leiv, and Diti
whose knowledge, dedication, and enthusiasm for South Georgia over nearly
twenty years of bold and meticulous exploration can never be equaled.

———————————

Copyright © 1998 by Tim and Pauline Carr
All rights reserved
Printed in Hong Kong

The text and display type of this book are set in Centaur

Color separations and manufacturing by Colorprint Offset Incorporated
Cartography by Jacques Chazaud
The photographs on pages 175, 176, and 177 are by Pat Lurcock
Photograph on page 244 by permission of *WoodenBoat* magazine

Book design by Susan McClellan

Library of Congress Cataloging-in-Publication Data
Carr, Tim, 1941 -
Antarctic oasis : under the spell of South Georgia / Tim and Pauline Carr ;
photographs by Tim Carr.
p.   cm.

ISBN 0-393-04605-2

1. Carr, Tim, 1941 -   —Journeys. 2. Carr, Pauline—Journeys.
3. Curlew (Yacht) 4. Voyages and travels. 5. South Georgia Island—
Description and travel. I. Carr, Pauline. II. Title.
G890.S58C37   1998
919.7 12 DC21   97-24636
                                                                CIP

W. W. NORTON & COMPANY, INC., 500 Fifth Avenue, New York, N.Y. 10110
http://www.wwnorton.com
W. W. Norton & Company Ltd., 10 Coptic Street, London WC1A 1PU

4 5 6 7 8 9 0

CONTENTS

FOREWORD

WILD AND INACCESSIBLE PLACES have always had a fascination for the adventurous. South Georgia is just such a place, but it also has an intriguing history. Cook and Weddell had a look at it; Shackleton owed his life, and the lives of his whole expedition, to it. For many years during this and the last century, it served as a base for whalers and sealers. Its most recent intrusion into world affairs came during the Falklands crisis, ending with a sharp action between a British warship and an Argentine submarine.

I was fortunate to have had a glimpse of this dramatically beautiful island from the Royal Yacht *Britannia* some 40 years ago, when the whaling base was still working and the whale-catchers still scoured the Southern Ocean waters for the ever-decreasing stock of large whales.

South Georgia deserves a book like *Antarctic Oasis.* The authors have captured the special qualities of this remote relic of a natural environment, which are rapidly disappearing from our heavily populated world. I will certainly never forget the snow-covered mountains rising almost straight out of the sea, the flocks of sea birds, and particularly the Antarctic terns, and the colonies of grunting elephant seals and the more delicate fur seals. This is just the book for all those with a taste for the unusual.

— H.R.H. THE DUKE OF EDINBURGH,
K.G., K.T.

PREFACE

THIS BOOK IS FOR THOSE OF US who grew up dreaming of a garden of Eden where you could walk unharmed among abundant and fearless wildlife in a beautiful wilderness — an oasis of serenity in a world increasingly out of step with nature. For twenty-five years our little sailing boat *Curlew* tracked across the oceans of the world and visited many countries, some with great individual charm. Always, though, we traveled on toward some elusive and ill-defined goal. More than a thousand miles east from Cape Horn and almost that distance northeast of the Antarctic continent, we reached the island of South Georgia and saw its awesome glacier-clad peaks rising steeply from the sea for most of its hundred-mile length. On closing with the coast the sounds and sights of tens of thousands of breeding birds and seals were overwhelming. We knew then that we had found the most exceptional place on earth. We fell under its spell and so here we decided to stay.

The childhood fantasy of Eden is surely a warm place where the sun could shine on bare skin — impossible here without a goodly layer of blubber, hair, or feathers. But the climate is still not so severe that we cannot survive and even live comfortably on our simple, wooden boat without recourse to a specialized, climate-controlled "base." It may be cold and rugged, with savage winds at times, but to us, warmly clad, it is an icy paradise.

South Georgia (the uninspired name was given the island by Captain Cook, the first human to set foot on its shores) is home to the greatest concentration of Antarctic and sub-Antarctic wildlife on the planet. If you were to count only the accessible coastal fringe in the summer, we doubt whether there is any land on earth which has such a density of birds and mammals. And the heartwarming miracle is that they are all approachable.

In summer there are 2.2 million fur seals crowding the shoreline; 95 percent of the world's population. They are constantly active even on land, fighting or playing, and surprisingly doglike with their ability to run on articulated flippers. In the sea, in their element, they are the ultimate in sinuous grace. By contrast, the slow-moving, ponderous elephant seals are the largest seals in the world, up to 17 feet long and weighing 8,000 pounds. The 360,000 that breed on South Georgia, more than half the world's population, are often packed into rows a dozen deep with up to 6,000 lying on one beach. They also gain a new dignity on entering the sea, but few people have ever had the chance to watch them in diving mode; they are able to swim to an ocean floor almost a mile deep, confounding marine biologists. Fur seals were threatened with extinction in the eighteenth and nineteenth centuries, and elephant seals were severely depleted. Both these species have returned to South Georgia in greater numbers than ever before. There are also small numbers of endearing Weddell seals and the rare chance to see the powerful, predatory leopard seal.

A little farther back from the hectic seal breeding beaches are close to 50 colonies of king penguins; the largest must contain more than 100,000 birds. With their glowing orange bibs and ear patches, these three-foot-tall creatures are surely the epitome of loveliness. But you wonder how their unruly chicks could ever make the transformation from gawky brown teddy bears to reach such heights of elegance. Climbing up to as high as 700 feet on the tussock-covered hills, you can find more than a third of the world's gentoo penguins in relatively small and peaceable groups of a few hundred each. Feisty chinstrap penguins extend the boundaries of their range to the southern coasts of the island, while high above on the most inaccessible, storm-lashed cliffs ten million macaroni penguins squabble over territories and gaze out from beneath golden crests with deep red eyes.

The largest number of wandering albatrosses in the world, perhaps some 8,000 birds, fly to South Georgia to nest where they can find the rare plateaux that offer enough runway space for them to take flight. This is a vital consideration for a bird with an eleven-foot wingspan. When a newly fledged bird flies for the first time, it will probably not return to dry land for another five years. In addition to the wandering albatrosses, a quarter of a million exquisitely marked smaller species — the black-browed, gray-headed, and light-mantled sooty albatrosses — nest on steep cliff sides.

There are millions of petrels and prions. Most of them live in burrows or crevices in the rock so that it is difficult to estimate their numbers. We have read figures from 5 million to 22 million birds. In winter the fearless skuas fly north, but we still have company from the ubiquitous shags, terns, and gulls. And there are three species that are not sea birds, though they also feed on the shore: sheathbills, ducks, and pipits, the tiny songbirds that lift our spirits in spring.

Only the whales are missing from this idyllic scene. But after sixty years of brutal exploitation and thirty of near-silence across the waters, there are now signs of regeneration and hope.

For five years this island in the Southern Ocean has been the stunning backdrop of our sailing, skiing, and mountain-climbing expeditions. Over half of South Georgia is covered with permanent ice and snow, and there are more than 150 glaciers, many of them disgorging millions of tons of ice into the bays. Some years the surrounding plankton-rich sea is dotted with larger icebergs carried north from the Antarctic mainland, slowly decaying, eroding, and capsizing as they drift toward their inevitable decline. The island's highest summit reaches to almost 10,000 feet and there are at least 300 peaks between 2,000 and 8,000 feet high, most of which have not been climbed or even named.

The extraordinary and sometimes hostile beauty of the inland areas has often lured us into the heights. But South Georgia has also turned a softer face toward us, offering indulgent, gentle strolls in warm sunshine along its emerald-fringed coast. For many people South Georgia is a holy grail — an almost inaccessible island, although cruise ships are now increasing and a handful of yachts make the journey each summer. Watching these people sail wistfully away, after just a glimpse of some of South Georgia's treasures, we realize what an immense privilege it is to live here permanently, the only people to do so. And it leaves us with a great desire to share our good fortune with other sympathetic souls. Perhaps you can come here to see South Georgia's charms for yourself, and come to understand why this place deserves care and protection. Even if that is not possible, we hope you can visit in spirit as you turn the pages.

— Pauline and Tim Carr, *Yacht Curlew*

ACKNOWLEDGMENTS

To Jérôme and Sally Poncet (*Yacht Damien II*) for urging us to write this book and for providing the initial inspiration. To Jennifer Elliott, Charlie Babb, Gail Anderson and Pete and Annie Hill (*Yacht Badger*) for encouragement and assistance with finding the publisher; Craig Shelton, assistant commissioner of the South Georgia Government for lending us his support; Pete Prince and Ian Boyd (British Antarctic Survey) for checking the accuracy of biological facts and observations. To Pat Lurcock (South Georgia Fisheries) for rescuing us from the willful whims of a steam-driven computer. To Sarah Lurcock for making many worthwhile suggestions while reading the draft of this book. And to both Pat and Sarah for their special friendship, sharing some of our adventures and enriching our lives in so many ways.

CHAPTER I

ULTIMATE LANDFALL

November 7, 1992

*F*LURRIES OF SNOW SWIRLED out of the darkness. Tim's eyes were straining with the effort of looking for dangerous pieces of ice amid the turbulent waves. He was hunched against the cold but then suddenly straightened up. "Yes!" he shouted to the unheeding wind, his voice a mixture of triumph and relief. Then he slid the hatch open and called down below from his chilly seat in the boat's cockpit. "Come

and look at this. I can see South Georgia." His words slowly penetrated my subconscious and I stretched stiffly within the confines of two sleeping bags and a blanket. Reaching for a lukewarm hot-water bottle somewhere down by my still-cold toes, I remembered where *Curlew* was. "Come and see, these must be the Willis Islands." Disentangling from the bed-

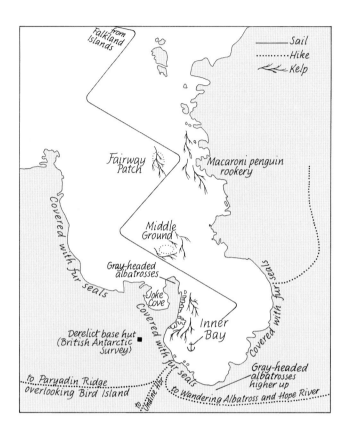

ding I turned up the oil lamp flame in the galley and then stuck my head out of the hatch into a wild, wintry night. Early November is spring in these southern latitudes but it could have fooled us. A late, waning moon was illuminating some high, snowcapped islands rising like steep ramparts into the dark, foreboding sky. Austere was the word that came to mind; even the lonely, windswept Falkland Islands seven blustery dawns astern seemed friendly by comparison.

A rainbow across Port Stanley had been our last sight of land, then strong winds and wet, gray squalls had enveloped us. *Curlew*'s decks, just 28 feet long and 9 feet wide, seemed a very tiny platform amidst the cresting waves along the route to South Georgia. Chains of cyclonic weather depressions sweep past Cape Horn; an intense one, not uncommon, generates huge, breaking seas which could easily capsize *Curlew*. As we crossed the Antarctic Convergence Zone the rain gave way to snow

ELSEHUL BAY

and the visibility decreased still further, obliterating the now numerous icebergs. We had to stop for several hours each night, heaving *Curlew* to, marking time under sail until the way ahead cleared. She had still gamely sailed over a hundred miles a day, a respectable average considering our necessary caution. This was not a good place for equipment failure and by our own choice we do not carry a radio or electronic beacon to "dial up a rescue."

Despite the frequent gale force winds and tumbling seas that often threatened to fill the cockpit, we felt fortunate that the notorious Southern Ocean had dealt evenhandedly with us this time. We still had vivid memories of our foray to the Antarctic Peninsula earlier in the year. Leaving the shelter of Palmer Base we had survived 48 hypothermic hours of storm-force winds, hanging on to life by a nervous thread as we steered the little cutter between enormous icebergs and their cottage-sized small sisters, bergy bits. More dangerous were the almost invisible semi-submerged growlers made of transparent ice, multifaceted and reflecting bottle green, that could easily splinter *Curlew*'s timber bow. The worst moment

had come when we were thrown bodily sideways by one rogue wave. Our little cockleshell was rolled over until the fiberglass dinghy strapped on deck was crushed and the mast pointed perilously toward the ocean floor.

There had been none of that life-threatening stuff on this journey, just plain rough, wet, and uncomfortable — but survivable.

In the predawn the boat felt very cold without the diesel heater. In heavy weather boarding seas can drench the fire below if we don't remove the smokestack and cap it, one of

Previous spread: *Arriving at South Georgia we were greeted by hundreds of icebergs of all shapes and sizes, decaying remnants of giant tabular bergs that had split from Antarctic iceshelves.* **Above**: *One hand for the ship and one hand for yourself — especially on a vessel without lifelines. Pauline tidying away loose ends as we approach the coast for the first time.*

many apparent shortcomings in taking so small and ancient a wooden craft "Southwards of the Usual Route of Vessels" — wording embossed on the front of the British admiralty's *Antarctic Pilot* (1974) which lay ready on the chart table.

Nevertheless, *Curlew* had looked after us for a quarter of a century. Although we might push her limits ever further, and despite her lack of an engine, she has such innate sailing abilities and seaworthiness that our confidence in her has never been misplaced.

I'M FAMISHED," TIM ANNOUNCED, as I primed the kerosene stove for tea and porridge. He clambered below awkwardly in his many layers of clothing and pulled off his snow goggles. "Any ice?" I asked. "Just a couple of bergs a fair way off, but I haven't seen any small stuff lately."

As the sky lightened the mainland of South Georgia lay white and stern before us. "Lands doomed by nature to perpetual frigidness: never to feel the warmth of the sun's rays; whose horrible and savage aspect I have not words to describe," is how Captain James Cook put it in 1775. Apart from a couple of accidental sightings during the preceding century, his visit with HMS *Resolution* was the first to discover and accurately map the position of the island.

"Primeval," said Tim, as he pushed the tiller and trimmed the sails to let *Curlew* romp away past Bird Island. Bird Sound was boiling with reefs and overfalls as we passed by. "I'm glad we didn't have to come through that lot!" Tim said, little realizing that over the years we would be regularly shortcutting through this "hazardous channel," as described by the *Antarctic Pilot*.

Across the sound the 1,500-foot-high Paryadin Ridge was disappearing into swirling clouds. Ahead of us lay a wall of sheer cliffs, their black faces veiled with fresh snow. Somewhere between them, we fervently hoped, would open up the entrance to Elsehul. This small, well-sheltered anchorage was perfectly positioned at the northwest tip of the island to give us a day of rest and adjustment, a decompression chamber from the stress of the passage.

The barometer started to climb and downdrafts of disturbed wind spun out across the water like miniature tornadoes from the southwest. Heeling sharply, *Curlew* sliced up into the wind and passed a fluted, grounded iceberg, the new snow turning it opalescent in the dawn light. Then the sun touched our world and a myriad of birds flew into it, the air thick with wings beating laboriously or held in stiff aerodynamic perfection.

As the sea became smoother, closer inshore, great rafts of black-browed and gray-headed albatrosses surrounded us. From a distance they appeared to be flocks of large, docile seagulls until they had to make an awkward and ungainly move out of *Curlew*'s track. Then powerful wings smacked into the water while large webbed feet ran across the surface. A hundred birds suddenly wheeled and circled back into their element, reaching upward to their cliff colonies 500 feet above us and lining our route. From high up there, too, came the haunting, exultant cry of the light-mantled sooty albatross, a call that will forever embody the essence of South Georgia.

One great wandering albatross passed by, aloof and serene, white body and wings making a gliding, gleaming cross. It was outlined against the angry dark sea that was becoming ever more distant and less fiercesome. *Curlew* slipped thankfully into safe waters.

We were approaching a rocky buttress still bathed in turbulent surf from the ocean swell. Dozens of macaroni penguins leaped out of the breaking waves onto a steep slab of stone and hopped up the winding tracks to a large colony above. With scant time to appreciate this amazing sight, and close to the surf ourselves, Tim spun *Curlew* on her keel as we tended the sails and lay a course across the bay. The inner harbor was marked by a peninsula covered with the nests of gray-headed albatrosses, looking like hundreds of alpine flowers amidst the vivid green clumps of tussock grass.

Tacking the boat across the bay again we saw that the approaching rocky shore was lined with fur seal bulls sitting in stone-statue poses. The strong musky smell of them wafted out across the water. Now *Curlew* was sailing through a patch of sheltering kelp, fronds spreading out on the surface of the water and further dampening the waves. On a gentle beach lay a line of large, inert bodies — elephant seals. Beyond the black sand was a dilapidated British Antarctic Survey hut, inhabitants long since departed, but with a crowd of gentoo penguins by the door and some king penguins keeping a dignified distance. One king penguin stretched its beak to the sky, swelling its orange-bibbed, satin chest, and trumpeted triumphantly as if to herald our arrival.

Our first good look at South Georgia's glacier-clad peaks and rugged shoreline.
Somewhere amidst these cliffs, we fervently hope, is the entrance to Elsehul's sheltered bay.

Tucking *Curlew* in behind a rocky spit that closed off the sea from our view, we dropped anchor. Tim paid out most of its 300 feet of chain, despite the relatively shallow depth of 20 feet that our hand leadline had registered. Overkill maybe, but we planned on sleeping confidently for a few hours snuggled together under the quilt in our double bunk, up in the bows of the boat. Tim came aft from securing the chain. His arms surrounded me in a great bear-hug and we stood motionless and entwined for a long, long time. Despite all the layers of waterproofing and padding between us, we had never felt closer.

Eventually we slipped apart. "Sail cover on?" I asked, knowing the answer as I went below to extract it from the fo'c'sle. Tim replaced the smokestack for the stove, lit it, and soon the metal turned cherry red as it roared into life with all the vents open. We watched in gratitude as our hands and faces absorbed the warmth, and then turned in for a few hours of oblivion.

The warm boat was blissful to wake to. The wind had eased and sunlight was streaming brightly through the three large hatches, lighting up the varnished oak frames and pitch pine planking. Bacon and eggs soon sizzled away in the frying pan and we ate sitting on our saloon settees grinning at each other with simple happiness.

B ACK IN 1980, AFTER SPENDING A DOZEN YEARS in Mediterranean and tropical waters, *Curlew* sailed beyond 40 degrees South, into the "roaring forties," for the first time. There we met the people who were to alter our way of life dramatically.

After cruising around the island of Tasmania during the summer and early winter we had hauled *Curlew* ashore for painting at the Royal Yacht Club in Tasmania's capital, Hobart. A big maroon schooner came in and tied up to the dock flying the French tricolor. *Damien II* looked nearly new, practical and workmanlike, but all the steel on her waterline was rippled like corrugated iron, with several really big dents.

We were washing *Curlew*'s bottom with a hose and hand scrubbing brush and I don't mind admitting it was a bit chilly in the wind with a stream of water running down her sides and then dripping all over us. Suddenly an accented voice said, "'Allo. We wonder if you like thees?" and Jérôme Poncet was standing there — bright eyed, olive skinned, and compact, with an aura of confidence, but no trace of conceit, and cradling a palm leaf basket full of coconuts and pamplemousses. "We breeng them from Tahiti — alors, do you not feel the

Joke Cove, in Elsehul Bay, teems with life in high Antarctic summer.
Pauline takes a closer look at elephant seals, fur seals, gentoo and king penguins from the dinghy.

cold?" A little irony, perhaps, for these were the people, we soon learned, who had just over-wintered in the Antarctic Peninsula, frozen into the ice for nine or ten months. Now the reason for that dented waterline became clear as we heard about *Damien II* bashing her way out from the pack ice before the next winter trapped her again.

Jérôme's beautiful Tasmanian wife, Sally, was serenely watching their young son taking early steps and splashing dirty puddle water all over his clean clothes. Dion had been born in South Georgia at an abandoned whaling station with only Jérôme to assist. Soon after, they had sailed for the Falkland Islands, Cape Horn, and then Tahiti.

A friendship was formed and the seed was sown as they described the wonders of the far south. They showed us photographs, even screened a film about their adventures. Our fascination for these wild places was growing fast, but we looked at *Damien II*'s big, tough steel hull, its powerful engine, and four-inch-thick insulation and the thought of taking *Curlew* there seemed far-fetched.

Since then, though, assisted by an extra layer of protective wooden sheathing, *Curlew* has proved her strength and abilities from New Zealand to Newfoundland by way of the Cape of Good Hope. Then from the Arctic Circle to the Falkland Islands at 52 degrees South. We spent the summer of 1991–92 treading the fine line between seamanship and high risk from Cape Horn to the Antarctic Peninsula. But South Georgia had always remained the ultimate goal, the very finest of high-latitude landfalls.

The Antarctic Peninsula, choked with ice, presents enormous difficulties for an engine-less yacht. *Curlew* is the only one as yet to have visited there, although the reason we sailed to Antarctica was never to be "the first" but rather a compelling urge to see the wildlife and beauty. We felt as though we had sailed off the edge of the planet to arrive at a surreal but nerve-racking and hostile fantasyland. In contrast, although South Georgia is more than half-covered with permanent snow and ice, we knew that between the high, crystal-topped mountains and tumbling blue glaciers there would also be many safe anchorages. And there, fringed by emerald tussock grass, we could relax and enjoy some almost balmy days surrounded by the plentiful wildlife.

All of the seals, birds, and penguins that inhabit the seas around Antarctica need to come ashore to breed. A few manage to do this on the ice but the vast majority look for solid ground, beaches or cliffs. Only a tiny fraction of Antarctica's coasts are not perma-

The brilliant orange ear patches and bib of the king penguin make it unmistakable and unforgettable. On South Georgia these handsome birds are unafraid of humans.

nently covered with snow and ice so most of the wildlife head toward the islands that form a tenuous ring around this frozen continent. Some lie to the north of the Antarctic Convergence, which is a fairly sharply defined line between frigid and more temperate seas. These are the sub-Antarctic islands such as Crozet in the Indian Ocean and Campbell in the Pacific. Others lie right on the line, including Kerguélen and Macquarie.

Some islands are much closer to Antarctica and get surrounded by pack ice with almost as severe conditions as the continent itself. But a very precious trio of islands south of the Antarctic Convergence benefit from the nutrient-rich cold seas yet have a relatively mild maritime climate north of the icy extremes. These are Bouvetøya, Heard, and South Georgia.

However benign the onlooking king penguins may be, there is no chance of landing here.
The fur seal bulls weigh around 400 pounds and will charge instantly, baring very sharp teeth.

The first two are wild, savage places — Bouvetøya is said to be the most inaccessible place on earth; certainly it is the most isolated piece of land on the globe. Neither island offers anything in the way of secure anchorages or sheltered beaches and have been visited only on rare occasions.

South Georgia in summer is different. It abounds in magnificent beaches that attract the elephant seals and king penguins; it has gentle tussock-covered slopes for the fur seals and gentoo penguins. There are surf-bathed cliffs dotted with tussock grass for the macaroni penguins and smaller albatrosses, and grassy runways on hilltops for the majestic wandering albatrosses and the giant petrels. Blue petrels, white-chinned petrels, diving petrels, and prions can dig their burrows into unfrozen peaty earth. Snow petrels and storm petrels find crevices and niches in the rocks of high mountains. Gulls, terns, shags, skuas, even ducks and pipits all find a suitable nest site in the garland of green that emerges from the spring thaws.

It is equally important for most of these creatures to have a nearby food supply, and this is also where South Georgia excels. Deep ocean currents and upwellings close to the Convergence Zone bring up phosphates and nitrates to feed minute plants called phytoplankton, which bloom near the surface of the sea in the long daylight hours of summer. The phytoplankton in turn feed the zooplankton, especially the shrimplike krill, which are the driving force of nearly all food chains. Krill grow to a maximum of 2 inches long but are generally smaller. Despite their individual size the numbers and mass are enormous — estimated to be trillions of animals with a total weight of 650 million tons. South Georgia generally gets more than its share of krill but occasionally the unpredictable currents and turbulent upwellings change their behavior and a season of famine occurs.

Summer 1992–93, however, was to be a particularly bountiful time. We were lucky to arrive at the height of spring when all the teeming activity was reaching a climax. As we got ready to go ashore our awareness of this dynamic breeding and feeding cycle made us all the more appreciative of what lay in store.

WELL, WHAT ARE WE WAITING FOR?" On deck the impact to our senses was almost physical. The braying and trumpeting of penguins vied with all the seal noises. Other seabirds were adding to the din and the small amphitheater of the bay concentrated it like a gladiatorial arena. Strange smells filled our nostrils made all the keener by a week away from land.

We launched the dinghy and rowed across the short stretch of water to the beckoning shore. As we paused a giant petrel, one of dozens sitting docilely on the water, paddled up with his enormous webbed feet and then curiously tested the oar blade with a powerful, hooked bill. So much for a notoriously timid bird.

The beach seethed with life. Every possible vantage spot was taken by bull fur seals waiting for the pregnant females to arrive during the next couple of weeks. And their numbers

stretched back into the hills, their silhouettes sharp against the distant sky. We were witnessing a miracle. Sealers, arriving a decade after Captain Cook, had all but exterminated the species. The tiny group that escaped the sealers' grasp had been slaughtered in the latter part of the nineteenth century. Yet over the past twenty or thirty years a staggering population explosion has occurred, a spectacular return to the previous numbers, or better. There were 1,600,000 animals by the 1990-91 count (by British Antarctic Survey scientists on board *Damien II*), an estimated 2,200,000 by 1996.

Tim looked for a landing place but as soon as we neared a seal's territory it would begin to challenge us, making a high, plaintive, whiffling sound, and brace on its fore flippers ready to lunge. On either side of it another 400-pound male would be waiting, their zones so finely demarcated that there was no place for a blundering human. Fur seals are agile with their articulated fore and hind flippers and cover the ground effectively and quickly. Their yellow fangs are so placed that they self-sharpen. We backed off.

How ironic to have sailed 10,000 miles only to be blocked on the beach by a determined wall of righteous seals. Although it was not altogether an unsatisfactory scenario to see humans held at bay for once from an animal's territory.

"Well, we've got to get used to them sooner or later," said Tim after some thought. "If you row me over to that corner I think I can reach the rocks and then gather my wits in relative safety."

*Above: A fur seal relaxes on a clump of tussock grass. **Opposite:** South Georgia's wide, sheltered beaches, a rarity in the Antarctic region, make them the breeding grounds for untold thousands of seals and penguins.*

He took a spare dinghy oar and stepped gingerly ashore. Immediately the closest bull lunged at him and Tim held out the spar toward the brindled chin, the long white whiskers nearly reaching the ground. Standoff. But already from Tim's other side another powerfully muscled male was threatening. Seal researchers explain that there is no need to hit or hurt the animals, that a touch on the chin with the end of a pole usually does the trick. That's a relief, we had thought, until they added that there might be a few times when a seal just keeps on coming! So Tim had to use his oar with the flair of a frightened duelist retreating before a hostile mob. He worked his way across the beach fending off outraged seals until he

Opposite: Main avenue through a macaroni penguin colony, with a constant flow of birds walking between the sea and their nest sites above the beaches. **Above:** *Toward the end of the breeding season (and the end of his prime), this old fur seal bull is barely able to open one eye for the camera.*

eventually reached the rocks where he could relax. For this was, apparently, no-seal's-land.

The fur seal "wigs" — the name given them by the sealers because their handsome grizzled manes resemble British court wigs — lost interest the moment Tim passed the exact bounds of their territory. They resumed their aloof poses, noses pointed skyward and eyes seemingly closed.

I watched Tim leave the rocks and head inland with progressively fewer attacks from the subordinate males who halfheartedly defended less desirable territories. For myself, I was content to row the dinghy along the shore and view the wildlife from a safer distance. At least I hoped it was safe. A large bull elephant seal, twice as long as the little rowing boat,

Prince Olav Harbour, site of a long-abandoned whaling station, is graced by the wrecked hulk of the sailing ship Brutus, *built in Glasgow in 1883.*

appeared off its bow and rolled on his side to fix me with bloodshot, calculating eyes.

It was several hours before I saw Tim returning. He had crossed the narrow neck of land that separates Elsehul from Undine Harbour on the other side of South Georgia. In 1823 Captain James Weddell had anchored there with his vessels *Jane* and *Beaufoy* after sailing to 74 degrees 14 minutes South in the sea that now bears his name. He was also a sealer and described how men would portage their heavy boats across the Elsehul isthmus to save the dangerous and difficult sail through Bird Sound.

Beyond this lay the Hope River and its long winding valley. Here, Tim reported, scattered about the hillsides wandering albatross chicks were earnestly exercising their 11-foot wingspans like small windmills in readiness for their first flights. Every ten minutes or so they stood up on their 18-inch-high pedestal nests, spread their downy wings through which the black flight

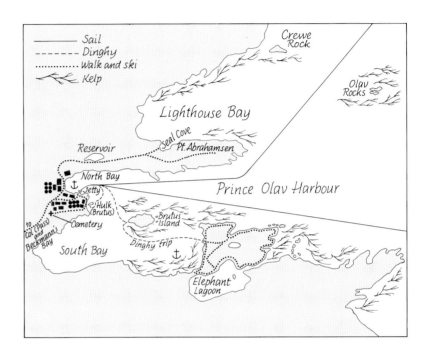

PRINCE OLAV
HARBOUR

feathers were sprouting, and then beat the air with all the dedication of Olympic athletes in training.

Towering above the whole incomparable scene was Snow Peak, 2,829 feet high, a cloud still lying on its shoulders but the sun lighting up the summit. Snow Peak is the northernmost of a succession of mountains that run the length of the island, almost 100 miles long, culminating in Mount Paget, 9,625 feet high. It lies roughly in the center and shields Cumberland Bay, where we were bound next day to be officially entered by the authorities at King Edward Point. Then to begin our jobs at the abandoned whaling station of Grytviken where a new museum was being set up.

We have returned to Elsehul several times since and in high summer have found the beaches even busier. Thousands of month-old black pups and many of the females — those not at sea feeding — add to the congestion and the clamor. In their midst once we spotted the most striking "wig" of all, a huge blond animal that looked more like a polar bear from a distance. One in a thousand fur seals is born a beautiful palomino color, darkening to a pale chestnut with maturity. Few ever reach the splendor of this senior bull, although we have seen a lot of younger adults and many exquisitely pale pups.

*C*urlew BOUNDED CHEERFULLY OUT TO SEA again in the early morning. Despite an overcast and windy start our spirits were high with the success of yesterday's landfall and the excitement of the long coastline stretching beyond us to the southeast. We felt that all South Georgia's treasures lay before us. Although we were tempted to start exploring each bay and cove, we knew that the harbormaster in the administrative center, 60 miles farther down the coast, would be expecting us. Weather permitting, we ought to sail directly there. But by midday we could see that a mile or two ahead of us the wind was lifting the surface of the sea into the great spiral swirls known as williwaws. Fear easily overcame any sense of duty and gave the excuse to shelter in one of the three bays at Prince Olav Harbour, just 35 miles from Elsehul.

"Well," said Tim, reading from the *Antarctic Pilot*, "the voice of doom doesn't give much to choose among these anchorages. It says that 'North Bay has winds attaining hurricane force at times but that at South Bay winds blow at times with great violence.' And East Bay is much too exposed to these winds."

"Whatever are we doing here?" I wondered, and yet the tense nervous pressure below my rib cage was vying with the adrenaline surge in my blood at the sight of such splendid glaciers and mountains. Tim was not exactly free of nerves himself; he just hid it better. And certainly this was the culmination of all his boyhood dreams, young man's enthusiasm, and now middle-aged determination to take *Curlew* and me on such an adventure.

Luckily this day the wind was confining most of its wrath to Possession Bay, 2 miles distant, where the water was being churned up to look like a stream of white smoke. Prince Olav was in a less savage mood so *Curlew* slipped quietly in to anchor off the derelict whaling station, abandoned in 1930. Just outside the cove the hulk of a stranded sailing ship graced the shoreline, rusting red in the afternoon rays. A spectacular, shark-fin-shaped mountain formed a theatrical backdrop as the sun moved slowly out of sight behind it and the chill of the night hurried us belowdecks.

A day later we spread all the sails to face the rising sun and continued east. A freshening breeze funneled out of Cumberland Bay West and *Curlew* lifted her matronly skirts and fairly skimmed across it and toward King Edward Cove. This inner anchorage was hidden behind a steep mountain which began to block the wind so that the pace was slowed. We didn't mind since it gave us ample time to savor the experience of reaching our new home.

Curlew at anchor at the abandoned whaling station at Prince Olav Harbour.
Hay Peak forms a surreal backdrop as the sun moves slowly out of sight behind it.

CHAPTER II

ANTARCTIC
OUTPOST

November 1992

*C*urlew's JOURNEY WAS FINALLY OVER as

we anchored off the abandoned Grytviken whaling station. For

a while we just sat on deck absorbing the impressive surround-

ings. The mainsail and topsail reflected in the calm water along

with the ring of mountains that dominated the whole picture.

The buildings of the whaling station spread all across the head

of the cove; a combination of rust red iron, bleached gray, and

faded ocher paintwork all blended smoothly together. The old whale oil tanks, blubber factory, chimneys, and stores looked as though they had all been spray-painted in one giant operation and from the distance the whole effect was surprisingly aesthetic.

One large white house stood out against the rusty background with its bright red, newly painted roof. A flagpole in front of it supported two rather limp flags, so this, we decided, would be the manager's "villa" where the museum was housed. There were three ramshackle jetties fronting the buildings so after a while we furled the sails, launched the dinghy, and Tim took a long line ashore. No easy motoring directly alongside, the price of not having an engine, but a slow and tiring haul until *Curlew* was close enough to be moored up properly for a well-deserved rest.

Although the station is now a heritage site and a museum, it was odd to feel that *Curlew*, still very serviceable, outdated everything we saw. The year of her launching, 1898, was six years before the whaling factory was built. What a beautiful, pristine place this must have been then, with whales cavorting in safety throughout Cumberland Bay.

Next morning we went ashore to meet our new boss, the project director of the whaling museum, which had only just opened earlier that year. Nigel Bonner's knowledge flowed as enthusiastically as his long white beard. "When the Swedish expedition ship *Antarctic* anchored in Maiviken Cove, four miles away from here, in 1902, and three of their scientists walked over the pass and looked down, they thought they were the first to discover this sheltered cove tucked almost out of sight of Cumberland Bay. Then they found these sealers' try-pots already on the beach." He took the weight off his walking stick and pointed with it to the big black pots. "So they called it Grytviken, which means Pot Cove."

These were displayed along with harpoons and other artifacts in front of the museum. "*Antarctic*'s captain, Carl Anton Larsen, recognized the value of the best anchorage in South

__Previous spread:__ Curlew sails into Cumberland Bay, entrance to our home waters, then tacks across King Edward Cove (__above__) as she nears Grytviken whaling station (__opposite__), with its red-roofed manager's villa, now home to the Whaling Museum.

Georgia with whales sporting within sight of the cove and came back with about eighty Norwegians to build the whaling station in 1904.

"Of course, the British, who had claimed the island since Captain Cook named it in 1775, renamed the cove in 1906 to honor their current King Edward. But 'Grytviken' has stuck for the whaling station and helps to differentiate it from the administrative settlement that was built on the spit of land across King Edward Cove in 1909 and called King Edward Point. The army has been there since 1982 and delight in shortening everything, so these days it is just KEP."

"Apart from the army, who else lives here?" we asked. "Well, you've already met the fisheries officer, who, acting as harbormaster and customs officer, cleared you in to South Georgia. Bob and Ian and myself, the museum team, will be here for two months, staying with the army at KEP, too. Bird Island is the only other bit of South Georgia to be inhabited year-round, by British Antarctic Survey (BAS) scientists. Usually there are just three of them, but a few more visit in the breeding season. Also at the moment there is a BAS summer presence at Husvik twenty miles away, but they are isolated from here by two virtually impassable glaciers.

"Very different to my early days here as a whaling inspector when there were over a thousand men working out of four whaling stations, and lots of boat activity between them all. No wonder they needed a magistrate to administer the place, one or two policemen, and even a jail! After the whaling days were over there wasn't much need for an administration so the British Antarctic Survey ran King Edward Point as a scientific station with the base commander acting as magistrate. Then came the Argentinian invasion in 1982 when the BAS people were captured and forcibly removed from the island. Since the island's liberation twenty-three days later, the army has remained here to defend it, and the officer in charge of the garrison is also technically the magistrate — but it's become rather an honorary posting now with really not much involved.

Opposite: The grounded whale catcher Petrel *with a waning moon over Grytviken.* **Above:** *The light-mantled sooty albatross is one of four species to live on South Georgia. This pair chose to nest in our neighborhood, overlooking King Edward Cove.*

"That's about it. When we leave at Christmas, you'll have Grytviken all to yourselves . . . and most of the island too, for that matter." He sounded wistful. "I do envy you. It's such a magnificent place. Don't get too bogged down with museum work." He smiled, with just a hint of conspiracy creeping into his voice, and said, "Use the good days for walking or skiing. They can be quite precious."

His eyes were very dark and shining. The aging frame and nagging hip problems were forgotten for a moment as Nigel relived some of his best days when he and a fellow scientist had spent over a year, 1953–54, at Ample Bay in the Bay of Isles studying king penguins. Then followed several years as government sealing and whaling inspector based at King Edward Point. Working intimately with the whalers meant that he understood the workings of the old whaling station and its ships better than any other person alive. He joined the British Antarctic Survey and went on to become head of life sciences and deputy director. Now in his retirement he had found further fulfillment in creating this museum.

He told us that he hoped it would cause visitors to think a little more deeply about the whaling industry, the management of natural resources, and the society of whalers, for whom he had great admiration as fellow humans, despite acknowledging the damage they had collectively wrought. But when Nigel left South Georgia, flying over Grytviken in a naval helicopter, it was for the last time. A year and a half later we received a message to say that Nigel Bonner had died of a massive heart attack.

NOW, OVER FIVE YEARS SINCE SOUTH GEORGIA first filled our lives with its grandeur and magic, it is difficult to relate to anywhere else so clearly and in the same positive light. This has become our real world while the madness that we occasionally hear about on the radio is a nightmare human creation. In all of our previous ramblings across the globe with *Curlew*, since 1968, we have seldom stopped for more than a year in one country, let alone a relatively small island. Perhaps this in itself explains what a spell the place has cast over us. And for those years Grytviken has been our home base, safe haven, and workplace. Walking the empty whaling station streets, detouring around slumbering seals, and conversing with the penguins as we pass are second nature.

The ghostly atmosphere haunted us at first, and we were uneasy walking alone after dark.

A pair of king penguins pose in front of the partially sunken steam sealers Dias *and* Albatros, *built in 1906 and 1921 respectively. Such remnants of South Georgia's whaling days are a stark contrast to the island's resurgent wildlife populations. They remind us of the horrors these shores have seen — the slaughter of nearly all of the great whales of the Southern Ocean.*

Eddies of wind whistle through deserted streets, sheets of corrugated iron flap and grate insistently, the windows of the manager's villa reflect moonlight and glow with an unearthly light. Doors open slowly on creaking hinges and then, caught by a gust, slam shut as though Olof the flenser or Karl the gunner has returned. With a northerly wind the overhead steam pipe moans as pervasively as the sound track of a Hollywood horror movie. But there is always a rational explanation for these noises and as the time passed so our familiarity overrode the prevailing eeriness.

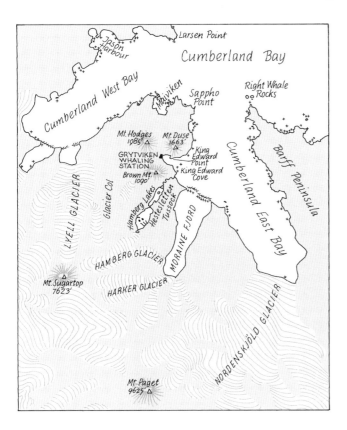

GRYTVIKEN AND
ENVIRONS

Grytviken was the first whaling station to operate in the Antarctic, in 1904, and almost the last to be closed, in 1965, with all its machinery, accommodations, stores, and tanks intact, operational and ready to reopen when the whales returned. But the whales did not return. Little by little the elements, the Argentine invasion during the Falklands War, the subsequent retaking and use by the British army as an exercise area, vandalism, and "souveniring" have taken their toll. In winter thick snows hide and soften the dereliction; in summer rapid thaws reveal an Aladdin's cave of discovery.

Just thirty years ago the tall chimneys were still belching steam, the great whale carcasses bled mutely on the wide, wooden flensing platform — the "plan." Chains, steam winches, and blocks and tackles helped dismember the animals while the bone saws, cookers, and centrifuges completed the butchery. The docks were busy and the half dozen whale catchers and three elephant sealing vessels bustled across the little cove, past the protecting moraine spit and out into Cumberland Bay on their ruthless hunts for the last leviathans.

Behind the station is the wooden Norwegian church, built in 1913. We ring the two bronze bells from the steeple occasionally, and the organ can be persuaded to resound across the rows of empty pine pews. Nearby the old cinema has collapsed onto the ground, sway-backed, like some hamstrung animal.

The steam whale catcher *Petrel*, latter-day sealer, lies at the oiling jetty. Her mooring lines are lifeless now as her keel is firmly embedded in the mud and her stern is unable to sink any further despite the seas that wash over it in an easterly gale. *Curlew* is made fast to her starboard side where many a slaughtered blue or fin whale has lain in the past. On what they saw as a successful foray, the hunters would tow several whales back from the killing grounds.

Their tails were wrapped in chains and hoisted close to the sides of the vessel, the giant bodies pathetically trailing along each side. But despite the lookout barrel aloft and the harpoon gun still mounted on her bow, *Petrel* will never kill again. Grytviken has become a museum to intrigue and horrify, to commemorate and to condemn, and South Georgia is now bathed in the healing balm of the new Southern Ocean Sanctuary for whales.

The view from *Curlew*'s mooring place is a mixture of immediate dereliction, you could almost say desecration, and then distant uplift and inspiration. We look beyond the rusty corrugated tin and encroaching, decaying buildings to the sheer and beautiful mountain immediately behind the station. There is a powerful impact from these conflicting images. With the choice of several routes to its scant 2,000-foot summit, Mount Hodges is not a

The harpoon gun still mounted on Petrel's *bows points ineffectively toward the mountains and will never kill again.*

difficult climb. Yet it towers tall and impressive in its many moods, whether uncompromisingly hard and black in the summer, ethereally gray after a fresh dusting of snow, or sparklingly, invitingly white in the winter wonderland that we relish for six months of the year.

Jérôme says he's climbed it in less than an hour," Tim encouraged. "Yeah, yeah, and knowing him it was just with his rubber sea boots on, too," I protested. "I expect he went straight up the front face and then skied down. But I'm not Jérôme and I don't think I'm going to make it. This scree is terrifying." I was crawling on hands and knees while Tim strolled on, trying not to be impatient. We had elected to follow what we thought was the easiest path, around the back, but I still found it difficult to get a good footing. "Perhaps it will be better if I wait until winter when there's snow?" I pleaded. "Look, it's easy. You can run down it," said Tim, demonstrating, and sending a shower of rock past me to roll on down for hundreds of feet. Gulp. South Georgia's mountains, for all their beauty, are mostly composed of rotten shale, which is more than likely to come away in your hand.

"Aren't those snow petrels?" Tim had seen something up toward the summit. Suddenly our attention was on four lovely pure white birds flitting around some ledges far above us and close to the summit. "I wonder if we can get nearer to them?" Maybe that's what made the difference because somehow, almost physically pushed by Tim and pulled by the magnetism of these birds, I made it to the top with shaky legs, climbing slowly, watching each step ahead of me and never daring to look either up or down. I certainly didn't want to think about how we were going to get off the mountain. On the summit I was able to cower behind a rough rock wall, gradually get my breath back, and then start to look around.

That was the first and hardest time, and there have been many trips up there since. Little by little my confidence rose until the steep scree held fewer fears, and together we have even taken a couple of routes up the sheerer front face of the mountain. And I have enjoyed it. The best reward was to see the snow petrels snow-bathing. Just like a city sparrow will take a dust bath, the dove-sized snow petrels play in the snow, shuffling their wings, turning on their backs and rolling in abandon in the fine white powder. Except for their black feet, black bill, and black eyes, they are almost transparently white. At sea they are nearly always

A view of Grytviken whaling station from the 1,663-foot summit of Mount Duse.
King Edward Point, in the foreground, is home to the British army garrison.
Mount Sugartop (7,623 feet) rises above all.

associated with ice but in South Georgia they nest high in the barren mountains, often far inland.

The summit of Mount Hodges gives a stunning 360-degree view. You can look almost vertically down at the whaling station, just a little cluster of rusty buildings. Across the cove to the east there are the red roofs of the old administrative center at King Edward Point, now accommodating fewer than twenty soldiers who maintain and defend the immediate area and change over with new personnel every four months. Any initial enthusiasm for the place generally wanes soon for the soldiers, who miss their families and city lives. Most of

Above: While the view from the Duse Ridge toward King Edward Cove was clear during one calm early morning hike, a mist-shrouded world greeted us over the saddle toward Cumberland Bay.
Opposite: Moonrise over King Edward Point.

them are incredulous that we could be so content in what, to them, is a desolate wilderness, a hardship posting from which they count the days until they can leave.

Also at King Edward Point is the old post office building, still used for that purpose, and the home of the marine officer. Apart from wearing the hats of fisheries officer, harbormaster, and customs officer, he is also the postmaster. When the six-month tour of duty falls to Pat Lurcock, he brings his wife, Sarah, and our small circle of kindred spirits is happily extended. With binoculars we can see if Sarah has hoisted the battered red safety helmet that means they have a message for us.

Another steep mountain, Duse, 1,663 feet high and rising to an impressive double pinnacle, overshadows the point. It blocks out all the sun for four months in winter until at last a tentative finger of afternoon sunlight reaches into the buildings, raising the spirits and dispelling the depression of dark days. It was not until we climbed to the top of the southern pinnacle that we knew for certain that the northern pinnacle was taller — the map has it the

other way around. The higher pinnacle is a much more difficult rock climb and Tim was really delighted to reach that summit.

Turning toward the south you can see the third mountain to enclose the cove. This is the unimaginatively named Brown Mountain, a mere pimple in South Georgian terms of 1,090 feet. The name is an accurate description during the summer months when it intrudes on the more lofty white landscapes. Beyond it lies the Hestesletten plain and the Hamberg Lakes and then the many great glaciers and snowfields rolling off the mighty Allardyce Range that forms the central part of the island's spine.

O N A PERFECT DAY THE COLD ATMOSPHERE is clearer than glass and the distant vistas lie within a lively imagination's immediate grasp. There is something sacred about the individual mountain summits, each with a clear identity of its own and often haloed with a feather-like wisp of cirrus cloud. Then, after you have climbed high above the sounds of the wildlife and the surf, it is easy to tune into the music of the mountains and imagine the deep and resonant sounds of "ohm" and "oohm" and "aaahm" as from some celestial temples vibrating in the almost painfully bright sunlight. And a sudden and massive thunderous roaring when an avalanche tumbles down some sun-warmed slab of mountainside does nothing to dispel the sense of presences deep in the heart of the island. Something primitive within our own hearts echoes to these sounds with an almost religious reverence.

We could also look across to the north and northwest where the glaciers lie that feed into Cumberland Bay West, turning the dark waters into milky turquoise with meltwater. Above them the snowfields reach up and blend into the sky and lead toward the untracked interior of an island barely touched by humans and only roughly mapped.

Within a few hours' journey inland we can reach into these remote regions and find unnamed mountains to climb and vistas apparently without end. There are glaciers to cross, sometimes on skis. Waterfalls plummeting into rivers and lakes in the summer and turning into spectacular ice sculptures in the winter. For people who were once described as never leaving the high-tide mark, we have indeed come a long way.

Curlew, alongside the whale catcher Petrel, *begins the day with a spectacular sunrise.*
This is Curlew's *most sheltered berth, and where she spends many winter*
weeks when we are not out in her exploring the coast.

CHAPTER III

NINE to FIVE

December–January 1993

AFTER CLIMBING TO THE EXALTED HEIGHTS

and places of serenity among the glaciers and crags, it is some-

times hard to come quite literally back down to earth and get

on with our day's work at the museum. But there are lots of re-

wards here, too, as we construct and lay out the displays, refur-

bish artifacts, and generally keep the place from falling down.

From the two exhibition rooms here when we first arrived, the

museum now has six, with more planned. The original six summer cruise ship visits have now reached twenty-two and it is a genuine pleasure to meet many of the visitors who have gone to such lengths and costs to get here.

A few of the visitors come by yacht. There are four or five large ones, based in South America, that occasionally visit during the summer with adventurous charter parties, mountaineers, or film crews on board. Also a couple of private yachts whose owners, like ourselves, have long nurtured an ambition to sail in these waters. But as yet South Georgia has not had more than six visiting yachts in one summer and "Grytviken Yacht Club" has few members.

Previous spread: Among our domestic tasks at Grytviken is repair and maintenance of the tiny church. During winter Tim hauls timbers to the church as he repairs rotten rafters. **Above:** World Discoverer *is one of some two dozen cruise ships that call at Grytviken during the summer months to visit the South Georgia Whaling Museum.*

We see *Damien II* every year. If we are lucky Jérôme's wife, Sally, and their three sons are on board, but *Damien* is frequently full to the brim with film crew, BAS people, or other charterers. Back in the Falklands, working on his windswept island sheep farm through the winter, Jérôme sometimes seemed to have lost the vibrancy that separates him from the rest of us mere mortals, even appearing a little cynical. The downside of his roller-coaster nature, perhaps, dull days full of drudgery after the addictive freedom of his summer sailing.

But in South Georgia or Antarctica he thrives on action, excitement, and adventure. And like the rest of that special breed of charismatic and original adventurers, he sweeps us all along with the activities of his full days almost as though they are being choreographed. Sometimes *Damien* intrudes softly into our consciousness — a silhouette against a snowy mountainside that is gone again before our skis can reach her. And then we find a bag of mutton and root vegetables from his farm slung onto *Curlew*'s side decks. A note from Jérôme to glory in a good day, a reindeer shot, some rewarding filming, and a mountain climbed before dusk.

At other times we catch *Damien II*'s lines when she comes to the dock full of stories and adventures. The adrenaline is still fizzing as Jérôme talks of some catastrophe narrowly averted, hitting rocks, going aground, losing the propeller but always overcoming any problems with panache. And all combined with a wry Gallic shrug, a gesture that explains better than dozens of words.

And in the evening *Damien* is like a magnet as we all invade her smoky aft cabin. Jérôme reaches into the bilge for cartons of good South American wine, home-smoked meats, maybe fresh reindeer liver pâté, and we listen and talk, absorbed in the Southern Ocean scuttlebutt and relaxing in the mellow ambiance.

During the two or three months of summer the museum gets help from a few others who come down from England. Everyone works long days when there are only two or three dark hours in midsummer and the bulk of the painting and outdoor work is done. We also run a small gift shop as well as an office and workshop, powered by a diesel generator that gives lighting and a spot of welcome heat.

But *Curlew* is still our home and we find her much more aesthetic and snug than any of

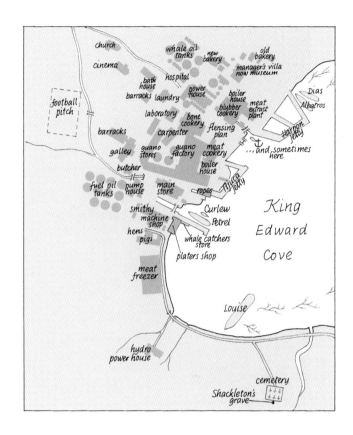

GRYTVIKEN
WHALING
STATION

the buildings ashore. Heating, lighting, and cooking aboard are all done by kerosene, which has to be shipped from Stanley, in the Falklands, along with the museum's hardware and paint supplies. Recently, though, we have been able to glean some out-of-date helicopter fuel when it has been replaced at King Edward Point, where it is kept for emergencies. Still, we are uncomfortably aware of our dependence on a nonrenewable energy source — six drums of fuel during a year can't help the environment we love so much.

I HATE SATURDAY MORNINGS," Tim announces, turning up with the sledge loaded with food stores. "I had a terrible time parking the car at the supermarket," he moans, trying to keep a straight face. "Yeah," I agree, suppressing giggles, "it wasn't much better at the Laundromat. I just couldn't get a free dryer." A silly little spoof, perhaps, but it is good to remind ourselves just what are the "convenient" alternatives of the "civilized" world. Laundry here is basic. We wash our clothes in hot soapy water left over from our

baths (which we take aboard the warm boat sitting in a large bowl of water filled by a kettle), rinse it in the nearby river, and hang it to dry in the old "guano store" for as long as it takes. In winter this can be a very long time. Often we have to bring stiff, frozen cardboard cutouts of our clothes back to the boat to thaw and dry finally in the heat of the stove, festooning the boat and making it look like a tenement slum. Likewise bringing water to the boat gets more difficult in winter when we sledge 20 gallons in jugs — about 200 pounds across the snow in a fiberglass pulk behind skis. Struggling to get the load moving or to back it out from the riverbank, it is easy to empathize with carthorses straining at their collars and slipping onto their knees — but the snow is mostly soft and the journey is short.

*Opposite: Pauline gathers dandelion leaves, one of the few fresh greens we gather throughout the summer. **Above:** Curlew, our home, is snug below-decks with the heater chortling away. The major of the army garrison is in for a treat of locally collected and caught food for dinner.*

As the first winter progressed I had to take an ice ax and hang from it in order to reach the water of the river because of piled high, frozen banks. It was time then to look for another source with easier access, even though it was farther down the bay. Happily, the fast-flowing streams that feed into the cove never freeze completely, although several feet of ice form on the lakes. The summer alternative to the sledge is an old whaling station wheelbarrow. This gets lots of use from early December, when the snows have thawed, until about May, when they usually build up again.

The mail service is best described as intermittent. It goes out by garrison supply ship about every six weeks but comes in by airdrop in between ship visits. Parachutes blossom from a low-flying RAF plane and the soldiers recover the sacks from the sea in small assault craft. Hazards besides high winds, waves, and ice in the bay also include people forgetting to waterproof the bags, parachutes that don't open, and insufficient buoyancy, but nevertheless the mail has always got through, for which we are eternally grateful. And when we put South Georgia stamps on our outgoing letters they often include pictures of *Damien II* and *Curlew*, as both were featured on a special stamp issue, to our immodestly great pleasure.

Most of our food comes by ship from the Falkland Islands when we can arrange for someone to buy it and send the boxes down. This is easier said than done, so we buy a year's supply of "hard tack" at a time when the opportunity presents itself. Tim has visited Stanley twice to do some work for the Falkland Islands Museum and brought back supplies; our stores nearly filled the empty swimming pool on a small cruise ship. Sarah is also a supremely efficient shopper and when we give her an ambitious list she rises to the challenge and manages to find lots of little luxuries hidden away on obscure shelves of the various Falkland Islands stores. Outdoor equipment mail-order catalogs do a roaring trade in Grytviken too.

All of our bulk food supplies are kept in rat-proofed shipping crates in the loft of the old whaling station "slop chest" (supply store). Until recently the rats were still able to live on the remnants of animal feed left in the station's piggery and other buildings. Although they can survive off the tussock grass roots, they are always on the lookout for something better and we have to be exceedingly careful not to encourage them.

Local fresh food is limited but very good and welcome as the first commanding officer of the garrison found one evening when we invited him to dinner. Cushioned by the central-

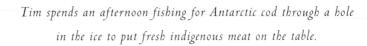

Tim spends an afternoon fishing for Antarctic cod through a hole in the ice to put fresh indigenous meat on the table.

heated comfort of his barracks, hot showers, and "french-fries-with-everything" cuisine, he accepted the invitation a little doubtfully, perhaps eyeing *Curlew*'s diminutive size. But the young major had been relieved to find *Curlew* warm and comfortable belowdecks, once he had run the gauntlet of two sliding hatches (our equivalent of double glazing to stop the in-

side one from freezing up) and the lack of a ladder to reach from the deck to the cabin floor five feet below. "Put your feet any-where. . .ah, but not in the frying pan." "Mind your head. . . ." We were a bit late with that one as he rubbed his forehead rue-fully. *Curlew* has substantial deck beams. "Watch the hot stove pipe" — he snatched his fingers away just in time.

"Isn't this nice," he settled back with a glass of well-chilled beer and placed his stockinged feet on the sheepskin rug, which was all that was insulating him from the re-frigerating bilges where the beer had been stored.

As I placed the raw fish appetizer on the table, Tim, who had spent the afternoon fishing for Antarctic cod, announced, "Indigenous food!" Actually, *Curlew* doesn't have a table, so we borrow the plywood wind vane from the boat's self-steering gear.

His doubts about the local first course may have been reinforced by what came next — squid rings (Southern Ocean, naturally) sautéed in butter and garlic. I thought the little curly pink tentacles gave a very decorative effect. Perhaps he was lucky we weren't serving him krill, another favorite.

He relaxed as the succulent steak course was served. . .until Tim mentioned reindeer. They are not indigenous — a small herd was brought here by the whalers in 1911. Since then they have spread and there are perhaps two thousand, damaging the vegetation.

Above: The gentoo penguin, like the larger king penguin, is a year-round resident.
The other species, the chinstrap and macaroni penguins, disappear out to sea for seven months of the year.
Opposite: South Georgia's weather is unpredictable, but tends toward cold. Yet in summer the strangely
warm fohn winds arrive, often bringing with them these lenticular (flying-saucer shaped) clouds.

The salad was not absolutely kosher either — another introduced species, dandelion. But here in the cold climate it grows more slowly than in other countries and is less bitter. "Where did you find this?" our guest asked. "In the graveyard," said Tim without thinking. "It's less likely that the elephant seals have been lying on it there." The major shuffled his salad uncomfortably around his plate. There were also a few tussock grass roots (sweet like chestnuts) and a few sprigs of a local burnet. This was highly praised by Captain James Weddell in 1823 when its antiscorbutic properties, along with roast albatrosses, helped his men to recover from their epic voyage to 78 degrees South. We do draw the line at albatrosses, though.

Above and opposite: Deep in winter much of the whaling station is buried in snow and we may not see the sun for days at a time. Yet it sometimes lets us know that it is still there in spectacular ways.

Warm, homemade bread eased the digestion of so many eccentric items. The accompanying wine, South African but purchased from an Antarctic research ship, had relaxed the major. He really enjoyed the dessert so we hadn't the heart to tell him it was made with abandoned king penguin eggs.

B Y CHRISTMAS THE ELEPHANT SEALS HAD LEFT and Grytviken seemed very quiet compared to the places we had visited on our sail down the coast. We were anxious to see more of the wildlife before the summer ended.

Grytviken lies in the central part of the coast and within a relatively deep bay, so it is not a particularly suitable place for fur seals and penguins, who need to reach deep-water food supplies as quickly and easily as possible from their colonies. One female fur seal has bred here in the cove for the past three years, but she seems to be unique. There is also one resident bull Weddell seal who harvests the Antarctic cod at night, under *Curlew* and *Petrel*, and then stretches out to sleep all day in sight of *Curlew's* berth.

Since there are no penguin colonies, we seldom see leopard seals, who also hang around where the food is, which often means penguin snacks. There are sometimes a few king penguins molting or the odd gentoo penguin resting overnight, but no large, breeding groups.

Only the elephant seals are not discouraged by the location — their priority is a good sloping sand beach for either breeding or molting later up among the tussock grass that backs the beaches. They fast for the whole breeding season and later during their molt, so in their case food supplies don't matter.

Three of the four types of albatross in South Georgia prefer the steady strong winds that they find at the ends of the island and off the western coast, so we do not see them at all near Grytviken. Only the light-mantled sooty albatross seems to have adapted to the more variable winds in the lees of the mountain ranges. In the past, we believe, they were driven away by military activity, gunfire, mortarfire, and loud explosions, which even frightened the less sensitive elephant seals back into the sea. This has stopped, after thirteen years, with the withdrawal of the infantry part of the garrison, and a few pairs are now breeding successfully locally.

As January approached we watched the weather with keener than usual interest since we were planning to leave soon on a summer cruise. South Georgia's weather is not at all predictable: It can go below freezing and snow during any month, though from late December through February the chances of bitter weather are reduced. Apart from weather recordings taken at King Edward Point for more than 60 years (until interrupted by the Argentinian invasion), there are no weather statistics for the island. Because of its sheltered position — we refer to the Cumberland Bay area as the "banana belt" — any readings from King Edward Point give a false impression for the whole island, where it tends to be very much windier and therefore feels colder. Minus 14 degrees Celsius (7 degrees Fahrenheit) is the coldest officially recorded here in July at sea level, although the army has unofficially recorded minus 20 degrees Celsius (minus 4 degrees Fahrenheit).

The strangely warm fohn winds are caused by a moist airmass being forced over the high

The deep snows of austral winter transform Grytviken, as they do our daily routines. Skis become our favored mode of transportation, both to explore the interior and to go "across town" to fetch water (carried in 20-gallon jugs on a pulk pulled behind skis) or to do the laundry. In winter this domestic task leaves us grappling with stiff freeze-dried versions of our clothes.

mountains that shield Cumberland Bays. Twenty-four degrees Celsius (75 degrees Fahrenheit) was the highest temperature measured one February, but we have sweltered in T-shirts in over 20 degrees Celsius (68 degrees Fahrenheit) on several days. This is a local effect not felt away from the lee of the tallest mountains and is usually accompanied by spectacular lenticular (flying-saucer shaped) clouds.

Whenever we go for a trip in South Georgia, either by land or by sea, it is a case of hoping for the best but always preparing for the worst. So it was with a little trepidation mixed with excitement that we readied *Curlew* for our first summer's cruise. The last tourist ship left in mid-January. We handed the museum keys to the marine officer and sailed *Curlew* out of the cove toward the south coast, hoping to find that both the summer weather and the breeding wildlife would still be with us.

South Georgia's weather keeps us guessing: It can go below freezing and snow during any month, though from late December through February the chances of bitter weather are reduced. It is always exciting to leave Grytviken for a cruise, be it summer or mid-winter, knowing that adventure is just around the corner. Calm, clear days like this can change to gales in a matter of hours, so we always hope for the best but prepare for the worst.

CHAPTER IV

GREEN ANTARCTIC

O VER TWO MONTHS HAD PASSED since we first tied *Curlew* up at Grytviken and our impatience to see more of the island had grown daily. At last Cumberland Bay East lay astern as we met the ocean swells again and slipped cautiously between the dubiously named Barff Point and Right Whale Rocks. The first and long since defunct lighthouse in South Georgia is a quaint, conical silhouette on the 90-foot

summit of the largest of these rocks. In December Jérôme had landed us on this tussock-covered hummock to give us the chance to see an island habitat where rats had not had their way. It was a very hairy landing in a high swell that bathed the shores with foam and our seaboots were filled as we struggled up the slippery, kelp-covered rocks. Gaining the grassy earth, it was alarming to find that every-where the ground was hollow beneath our feet, honeycombed with thousands of bur-rows. Jérôme opened one to show us the gentle, soft-plumaged adult bird which just blinked in the light without protest. Then he replaced the bird quickly and covered it up again. This was the only time we have seen a live dove prion so close, but despite Jérôme's scientific justification we felt like trespassers and were happy to go back to the slippery rocks and return to *Damien II.*

Right Whale Rocks dropped astern as *Curlew* flapped her way in a diminishing breeze for 5 or 6 miles farther down the coast. We kept a careful lookout for three breakers marked on the chart and, sure enough, their angry crests broke intermittently in the disturbed sea. Hoping for calmer water we sailed inshore between two reefy islands called West and East Skerries.

"Cobblers' Cove it is then," it was agreed, as the breeze dropped to a mere sigh and made further progress unlikely. With her big old-fashioned topsail set above the mainsail the canvas grabbed what desultory airs there were and *Curlew* headed for a break in the cliffs. There was certainly no turning back as the ocean swells all but washed her through the narrow entrance. "There's a rock dead ahead!" I shouted — but the rock submerged slowly and melted away — just an elephant seal. However, a real and uncharted reef did break deceitfully through the

*Previous spread: Cobblers' Cove, one of the most sheltered small boat anchorages in South Georgia, got its name from the white-chinned petrels that nest there. Here a pair is making the noise that gives them their nicknames: "cobbler" or "shoemaker." A hike out from the cove leads to a favorite nesting ground for macaroni penguins. By the time they are a month old (**opposite**), macaroni chicks begin to gather in groups or "creches." Colorful crests (**above**) are shaken during ritual mating displays.*

kelp as Tim turned *Curlew* back into the center of the cove and I let go the anchor.

The plan, this first summer, was to cruise toward the south coast of the island where we hoped to see the only colonies of chinstrap penguins in South Georgia. Already the weather had shown its fickle face, which was to make the round-trip journey of 120 miles last for

about a month. Tim characterizes South Georgian cruising this way: "If it ain't blowing hard 'tis rowing hard." But we were more than content to anchor in this beautiful small basin only 11 miles from Grytviken.

"Cobbler" is a nickname for a type of bird — white-chinned petrels otherwise known as "shoemakers" because of the chiming noise they make at the entrances to their burrows at night, which sounds like an old-fashioned cobbler at work. As the daylight faded the hillsides rang with this sound. There are said to be about 2 million of these powerful, compact black birds in South Georgia alone. In some cases you have

to look very hard indeed to see the white chin — just a few feathers beneath the pale greenish beak. Although not quite 2 feet long, with a 5-foot wingspan, they are better able to defend their burrows from introduced rats than the smaller petrels, so we are able to see, and hear, them on the mainland.

Light-mantled sooty albatrosses flew around the cove in perfectly matched pairs. These two-tone cocoa-brown and ashy-gray birds are almost 3 feet long with a 6- to 7-foot wingspan and a streamlined wedge tail. As their lifelong partnerships progress toward mating so their aerial coordination becomes more exact until they seem to be two graceful, aerodynamic bodies with but a single mind. The next day their ecstatic cries led us to cliffy nest sites to marvel at the big, beautiful birds with their wide-awake, startling white-ringed eyes gazing unafraid at perhaps the first humans they had ever seen close at hand. "Look. There's

Roughly 5 million pairs of the tough little macaroni penguin inhabit South Georgia.
Most live on cliffy offshore islands or above inaccessible beaches, so we were pleased to find
*a colony not far from Cobblers'. **Above:** A peck that says: "You are too close to me."*

a fantastic blue stripe running down its bill." Tim had noticed a subtle detail in the ebony perfection of the powerful beak.

It was warm in the sun with no wind and the little bowl of a bay was magnifying it. We wandered on among the waist-high tussock grass, occasionally pulling out the odd root to nibble on. Higher up the hillside, mosses reached an almost iridescent intensity and then the verdant growth stopped and rocky scree took over. We climbed a steep, snow-filled gully to reach a pass and were soon descending into Rookery Bay, where we followed our noses to discover a busy colony of macaroni penguins preoccupied with each other and their chicks to the total exclusion of the two large and lumbering observers.

Red eyes and golden crests make these little, 28-inch birds quite spectacular. Their efforts at leaping out of angry seas onto slippery, rocky ledges and then climbing high up a dauntingly steep hillside with stumpy bright pink legs fill us with admiration for their tenacity. Roughly 5 million pairs live in South Georgia (imagine trying to count them), but most inhabit sheer cliffy offshore islands or dangerous, inaccessible surf beaches, so we were delighted to see this colony so easily. Unlike the gentoo and king penguins, which can be seen in South Georgia year-round, the maca-

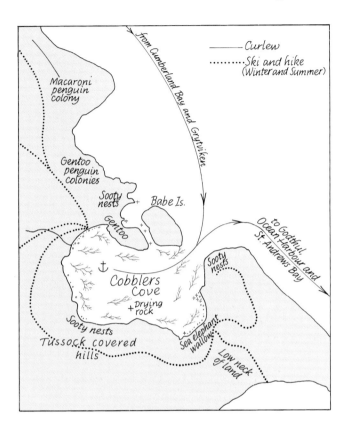

COBBLERS'
COVE

roni and the chinstrap penguins disappear out to sea completely for seven months of the year.

Macaronis lay two eggs but only the second, larger one is said to hatch. Yet we have seen and photographed quite mature "twin" chicks being protected by parents. Since they gather together soon after this stage in creches, or nurseries, it would be hard to prove that two offspring can really be raised successfully. Unless we were to mark them and interfere — something better left to the professionals of the British Antarctic Survey.

Macaronis eat krill and fish, and their heavy bills perhaps indicate a liking for larger crustaceans as well. There is a niche for each penguin species, because each feeds at a different level or distance out into the sea and on different-sized stages of krill, squid, or fish. Sometimes a catastrophic year occurs, such as our second summer of 1993–94, when virtually all fur seals and king, gentoo, and chinstrap penguins failed to raise any offspring in the absence of krill. Yet the macaronis, which feed on a different stage of krill, were able to go about business as usual and we were happy to see apparently full colonies and watch fat chicks being fed.

The origin of the name "macaroni" is curious. Apparently it comes from the old "Yankee Doodle Dandy" song — where he put a feather in his cap and called it macaroni. In turn this is said to have derived from the habit of eighteenth-century British dandies to do the grand tour of Europe and return with a dyed blonde or golden streak in their hair, as was the fashion among Italian men at the time.

It was only 7 miles from Cobblers' Cove around the distinctive sugarloaf mound of Cape George to Ocean Harbour, and yet here we found another world. Mist had shrouded the coast and it was difficult to be sure of the entrance until the breathtaking sight of a three-

It is only 7 miles from Cobblers' Cove to Ocean Harbour, yet here we find another world. From high up on the hillsides above the long-abandoned whaling station we can see icebergs scattered as far as the horizon. Nearby ones are stranded, the rest are marching slowly by.

masted bark hove into view. Bowsprit rigged above a clipper bow, masts all standing with topmast rigging attached to the trestle trees, she was slightly inclined toward us as though heeling to a fair breeze. This was the *Bayard*, one of the earliest remaining iron ships, built in Liverpool in 1864 and wrecked in Ocean Harbour in 1911 and now firmly aground with her bottom plating pierced by a pinnacle rock. We sailed past her stern, high above us, complete with a rudder still hanging from its fittings.

Bayard is one of the few items to remain from another whaling factory that was dismantled in 1920 and whose buildings and machinery were taken elsewhere to be reused. Where

---

Above: Bayard *was built in Liverpool, England, in 1864 and wrecked at Ocean Harbour in 1911 when hurricane-force winds blew her across the bay, wrenching her from the dock where she had been moored.*
Opposite: King penguins are unconcerned by our presence as we look across Ocean Harbour to the wreck of the Bayard.

there wasn't enough money to be made in relocating it, the scrap has been left to contaminate the otherwise pristine shores. Among the few other relics here we found a railway locomotive lying on its side with a bright-eyed fur seal pup in the firebox.

Two years later, in January 1995, an easterly gale brought huge breaking swells across the entrance that deposited piles of sand in the mouth of the river, causing it to break its banks and change its route to the sea, and new treasures were revealed. Tim found a delicate early-eighteenth-century glass bottle and I discovered a leather bucket, riveted with copper through brass bands and still watertight to this day. These must have been left from a sealers' camp. The earliest known grave in South Georgia is here, that of Frank Cabrail, steward aboard the U.S. sealer *Francis Allen*, who died 14 October 1820. Another grave, which contained a skull with a bullet in it, was unearthed by the whalers who came in 1910. A try-pot, periodically covered and uncovered by the shifting sand, lies in the southwest corner of the beach.

OCEAN HARBOUR IS A PARADISE, a safe harbor apparently shielded from the worst of the vigorous weather by the lay of the land. But the essence of cruising is adventure, so a few mornings later we sailed out and headed southeast once more. An amazingly multicolored dawn perhaps should have forewarned us, but *Curlew*

sailed serenely on. Later the approach of fine cirrus clouds steadily veiling the sun made bad weather almost a certainty so we were drawn to St. Andrews Bay, where, we had learned, some 100,000 king penguins were breeding. A cacophony of trumpeting adults and whistling chicks assaulted our ears while the strong smell of guano attacked our nostrils.

The barometer plummeted and we rode out a moderate gale overnight at St. Andrews Bay. By the following afternoon, a big swell broke on the 2-mile-long beach that fringes two receding glaciers, the Cook and the Heaney, but the front seemed to have passed with little ill effect. In the northwest corner of the bay a projecting reef offered some protection and a possible landing spot, so we launched the dinghy, keen to go ashore.

We were poised beyond the breakers while Tim judged the best moment to commit the little boat when something made him glance across to the other end of the bay. A huge spiral williwaw was churning a savage path out to sea. "Row back fast," he urged and, taking an oar each, together we struck out for *Curlew*. There was no way we could have rowed against such a wind if it had reached us. I tumbled onto *Curlew*'s deck while Tim quickly tied the oars into the dinghy. Together we slipped it up and over the side of the boat and flipped it upside down. By the time we had tightened the lashings the first blasts of wind hit, making us crouch low. The onslaught brought with it the moraine dust and penguin feathers that were to be plastered all over *Curlew* before the night was out.

Above: There are still a few cast iron trypots left on the beaches of South Georgia, macabre reminders of the elephant sealers who used them to render blubber into oil. Opposite: The cemetery at Ocean Harbour is the site of the oldest known grave on the island, that of Frank Cabrail, a sealer who died in 1820.

We watched a river of smoking water pour out of a distant valley and then steadily broaden to include us, tailing the little cutter back onto two of her three anchors. The rocks of the reef that had protected us earlier were now dangerously close to our stern. If both of the anchors had dragged, the rocks would have claimed *Curlew* immediately. Back at King Edward Point, we later learned, phenomenal winds of 115 knots (hurricane force is 63 knots) were being recorded and half the new boathouse roof was blown away. There was no sleep for us that night as we lay fully clothed, stiff with fear. We put all our documents and money into a waterproof bag with assorted survival equipment. Tim crawled on deck to check that nothing was chafing on our anchor gear. He wore ski goggles as protection from the stinging dust and whirling feathers. By 3 a.m. he thought there was a reduction in the wind, "but maybe we're just getting used to it," he qualified.

Nevertheless, dawn did follow the restless, lurching night. Subdued and numbed we thanked our lucky stars that daylight showed our bearings had not changed and for the

tried and tested anchors and lines that had not let us down.

During the day the storm became a gale, and then a breeze. In the evening we pulled up one anchor, ready for an early start. Unbelievably, by dawn the barometer, which had rebounded like a yo-yo, was on another downward roll. There was no wind for sailing, but both of us felt we couldn't endure another such storm in so vulnerable a spot, so we hurried to take up the remaining anchors and then Tim wielded the 14-foot oar to take *Curlew* along the coast toward the headland. Both of us voted to sail back to the safety and serenity of Ocean Harbour. There was a nasty sea running as we left St. Andrews Bay and scarcely enough breeze despite putting up every scrap of sail we had. My stomach was knotted with apprehension and nerves made me clamp my jaw till it ached. What wind there was soon resolved into the northwest — against us, of course — but *Curlew* has an uncanny knack of

"making the best." Within a few hours, and with the barometer plummeting all the while, the welcome silhouette of *Bayard* was in sight just as the first new williwaws came slithering ominously down the coastal cliffs.

Reducing sail quickly to the minimum we made it into the safety of Ocean Harbour. Even here, shortly after the anchors were down in two patches of sand between columns of kelp, the wind blasted and sang in the rigging. But it didn't have the menacing tone of the previous blow and we were soon able to relax again and count our blessings.

Not surprisingly, we took to the land for the next few days and hiked in several different directions. Johannsen Loch is an ethereal place where three waterfalls plummet 500 feet down the cliffs, draining meltwater from the icecap a couple of thousand feet above. The waterfalls have barely time to hit the rocks before their fresh water is mingling with the sea.

*As we weighed anchor to leave the safety of Ocean Harbour, a multicolored dawn should have forewarned us of more bad weather. Later in the day, the arrival of fine cirrus clouds veiling the sun (**above**) made winds and rough seas a certainty, so we made for nearby St. Andrews Bay. Sure enough, the barometric pressure plummeted, and that night we rode out a moderate gale.*

Penguins and fur seals played on the shore while sooty albatrosses flew over the cascades.

Tim was convinced he had found fish in one of a series of little lakes and went back with a sampling jar excited at the thought because there are not supposed to be any freshwater fish in South Georgia. He was disappointed and could only find amphipods, small freshwater crustaceans, and I laughed and mocked at there being no "Guppy carrii" to be named after him.

MIDSUMMER WAS PAST but the hillsides still looked green. The tussock grass was the predominant feature. Its tall swordlike leaves are often several feet high, but these grow out of a pedestal of old leaves and roots, making the plant really tall. Especially if the ground between the tussock plants is eroded by seals, it is possible in some places to find the leaves almost reaching head height. The reindeer and rats thrive on the roots and without tussock would probably be unable to survive here. Between the clumps there is generally burnet and a few other species of native grasses. The burnet has perfectly rounded red flowerheads held stiffly from a tall stalk that bobbles in the breeze. They contrast beautifully with the blue-green foliage of the plant and you can see great "fields" of it in some places. As autumn comes, the flowers turn brown and become seeds and then the plant shows its infuriating side. Little hooks develop on each seed, still in its collective round ball, and as you walk through the grass, which is virtually unavoidable, the balls attach themselves to your bootlaces, socks, trouser legs, or any other part of your clothing that you inadvisably let make contact. These burrs stick on seals and birds alike and are dispersed efficiently this way. Only the reindeer have learned how to cope with them. They eat the plant, seeds and all, and eradicate it. End of problem.

After several days of sailing amidst wild weather, we returned to the safety of Ocean Harbour, happy to explore terra firma.
Opposite: *Warm summer weather, melting the icecap 2,000 feet above Johannsen Loch, creates three waterfalls that plummet 500 feet to the beach.* ***Above:*** *Purple laver seaweed, washed ashore and blown onto the moss, makes a striking contrast.*

The reindeer don't seem to touch the beautiful emerald mosses, though. One type of moss (there are 125 species) changes color in the autumn ("fall" might be inappropriate, since we have no leaves to fall here) to a vivid burnt orange. Although the mosses aren't as slow growing as some farther south in Antarctica, we still try to avoid treading on them and leaving a footprint that will last for years.

Quaint, tiny red fungus disks grow in a few swampy places, and there are both white and brown toadstools. When we asked Jérôme if they were edible he tried a couple, spat out the brown one and then declared "the white ones are okay, but the brown ones taste bad." Armed with this in-depth study we have not risked it for ourselves — they are very small anyway. But Tim found some delicious lichens on the south coast and has been sampling them ever since, never to find the same species or stage of development twice. There are about 150 species plus 85 species of liverworts. Reindeer also find these lichens delectable and have virtually eliminated them from the areas they graze. There are a few ferns and even flowers too, Antarctic buttercups and Antarctic pearlwort, but like most of the less common flora they are so small and well hidden that you need to concentrate hard to find them. Very occasionally we have been drawn to the minute Antarctic bedstraw by its perfume — the only scented plant to be found on South Georgia.

Ocean Harbour is home to one of our (and Jérôme's) supplies of dandelions, which must have escaped from imported soil at the whaling station. Large clumps with delicious large and sweet leaves are hidden away in an elevated cave where the reindeer can't climb. We fill plastic bags to keep in *Curlew*'s cool dark bilges and give us salads for the next couple of weeks.

Adrenaline is like a favorite dessert—you can always manage just a little bit more. This

The summery side of South Georgia. These meltwater lakes and streams
are common around the coast, where the water must be the purest on earth. Burnet,
with their red flower heads (above), mosses, and tussock grass are in full flourish.

time, after a week in the harbor, the kelp had collected around the anchor chains and warps and it was a slow and tedious job to cut it all away. We then set our course for the southeast.

As *Curlew* approached Royal Bay, 15 miles farther down the coast, we faced yet more violent winds. Here they funnel right across the island through the Ross Pass and between 6,000-foot mountains that act so much like rocky walls that one is called Smokey Wall. For 6 miles we were hard pressed with short, smoking seas rolling across *Curlew*'s decks. But with more than 6 feet of boat and keel beneath the waves, she held her course resolutely and was soon in more sheltered waters where there was only a light breeze. Tim was laughing and shaking his head with disbelief, partly in reluctant admiration for the extreme forces of nature but probably mostly in relief that these forces had been so short-lived. A glimpse of the steamy mouth of hell for an hour at most.

Six and a half miles farther along, Gold Harbour offered us shelter for the night. The scenery was particularly beautiful and green, with rolling tussocky hills to the north and a blue glacier entering the sea to the south. Heavy clouds deprived us of an even more spectacular view. Just one bergy bit about the size of a bus was grounded on the 6-fathom mark, rolling uneasily in the constant swell, its stark white spurs and crests scooping up the turquoise meltwater as it lurched from side to side.

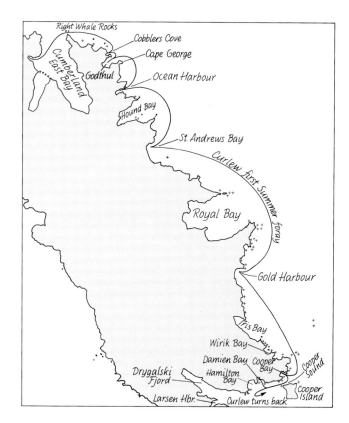

SUMMER 1993
CRUISE

A loud crack resounded as a section of the berg broke away. Now that it was lighter it could float free of the black beach, but since the wind was blowing away from us we assumed it would soon drift clear and sat down to enjoy a well-earned dinner. Suddenly there was a fizzing, crackling noise as millions of tiny, ancient air bubbles were released by the melting ice. Peering out of the hatchway we saw that our bergy neighbor was intent on paying us a visit. Icebergs move with the currents, not the wind; we should have remembered that.

Icebergs large and small are almost constant summer companions (or threats).
We found this impressive berg at the start of our summer cruise. Later, we ran afoul of a
bus-size berg that, moving on currents while we were at anchor, threatened to crush our rudder.

There was no time to move under sail so we pulled up on the anchor until it was barely still hooked on the bottom and hoisted the mainsail to take the weight off the chain. This moved us forward just enough for the berg to pass astern of us. But for a few tense minutes the glistening monster dipped and rolled, leaving perhaps a yard or two between its rock-hard spurs and *Curlew's* vulnerable rudder and self-steering gear. The boathook in Tim's hands was a feeble gesture. I felt shaky, but Tim was not too concerned, merely muttering, "Why do these things always happen in the middle of a meal?"

Gluttons for punishment, we plotted a course for Cooper Sound on the southeastern tip of the island. We had hoped above all to visit the chinstrap penguin colony there, the only one on South Georgia and the farthest north that these birds ever nest. But hard winds, fierce currents, and tumbling waves brought us to an anchorage that proved untenable in the swell. Icebergs encumbered the restricted waters and then yet more destructive winds funneled out of Drygalski Fjord.

But there were spectacular sights through the snow and spume: Groups of ghostly snow petrels flitted about the masthead as though trying to land, and chinstrap penguins surfaced all around us calling sharply to one another. We were thwarted at not being able to reach their colony but consoled ourselves with having seen it from a distance and promised to return one day in better conditions.

Already mid-February, it was time to turn around and head back up the coast. Ocean Harbour beckoned to us languorously again as the summer's adventures drew to a close. Our consciences told us that it was time to hoe into the job list at Grytviken. We moored *Curlew* back alongside *Petrel,* collected the mail and the museum keys, and went to work.

"It's still a pity about the chinstraps," I said, always greedily wanting cakes and halfpennies.

Breakfasting two days later we heard the unmistakable *aaark* of a chinstrap penguin. First looking incredulously at each other and then both bolting for, and squeezing into, the hatchway, we saw a solitary penguin emerge onto the slipway astern of *Curlew,* shake himself, and make a tour of inspection of the old timbers and rusting, decaying debris while calling continuously. It was hard to resist "aaarking" back at him, upon which he seemed quite satisfied with his incongruous surroundings and settled down for what was to become a three-week molt.

The slipway offered a nice hidey-hole out of the rain and snow and wind. Midway through his molt, just as his most inelegant moments were upon him, we heard another *aaark* coming from the distant shores of King Edward Cove. With mounting excitement the *aaarks* became louder as the newcomer zeroed in on the familiar-sounding beacon and leapt onto the foreshore. But although within a few feet of each other, the structure of the slipway caused great complications and a lengthy hide-and-seek exercise. Eventually the newcomer discovered an accessway so that all barriers were overcome. At last the two small figures, no more than 28 inches tall, stood beak-to-beak.

Penguin number one was so overwhelmed that he soon presented the newcomer with a fine collection of carefully selected stones. We presumed that this was courtship behavior by two immature birds practicing for next year when it would be their turn to breed. But then again it might have just been a nice penguiny gesture of friendship. The two birds stood side

Pauline tows Curlew *out of the way of a bergy bit that comes to share an anchorage. Natural sculptures of unique beauty from a distance, up close they pose a grave threat to* Curlew's *wooden hull. A few gentoo penguins are riding on the ice.*

by side for another week until eventually the first was sleek and handsome with only a couple of old feathers still sprouting from his new black plumage.

Then we all heard a third *aaark*. Tim added his insistent and apparently successful mimic to encourage the latest arrival. There were further responses and much strutting in fine style

as a pecking order was established. Three chinstraps in molt do not make a colony, but this was better than we could ever have imagined; on our doorstep, so to speak, a welcome sight just yards from the cockpit. Even on bad days we could observe them from the shelter of the hatchway.

By now the original duo had begun to take gentle swims around *Curlew*, flying beneath her in the clear, kelp-streamered water. Since their diet is almost entirely krill, they were probably not foraging trips. One day the pair did not return to the shore, their cries fading into the distance of Cumberland Bay and the open sea beyond.

The third chinstrap stayed with us until summer was but a memory and a couple of navy ships had visited, their successive, noisy crews joking and stamping loudly across the wooden slipway. They were watched from a dark recess by an amber-colored, olive-shaped eye in an anxious little white face, but the chinstrap was far below the line of the sailors' sight and so went unnoticed, sharing a special secret with us. *Aaark!*

Disappointed at failing to get a close look at chinstrap penguins at Cooper Sound, site of their only colonies in South Georgia, we reluctantly ended our summer cruise and returned to Grytviken. There, to our amazement, one, then two, then a third chinstrap arrived and settled in for several weeks to molt, just yards from Curlew's *cockpit.*

CHAPTER V

KINDRED SOULS

April 1993

A MONTH LATER WE WERE HAVING COFFEE in the back room of the museum. "There's no hardwood left in Grytviken to make cabinets and picture frames," said Tim with a grin. "We'll just have to go to Leith and find some there." "Oh dear. What a shame!" I was rejoicing at the more or less genuine excuse to go for another trip. "We can visit with the BAS folks at Husvik before they get taken out by their ship. Maybe we can also find some more artifacts there for the museum before the snows cover everything up."

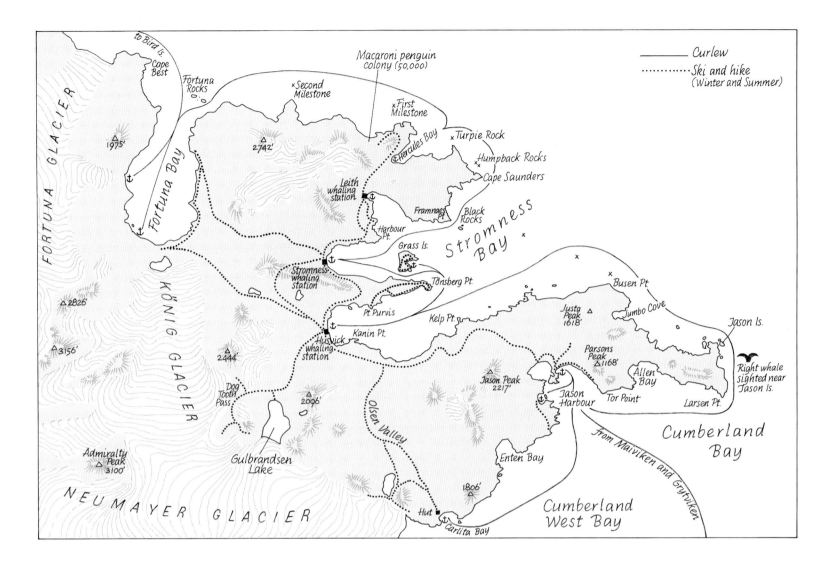

Map labels:
to Bird Is.
Cape Best
Fortuna Rocks
FORTUNA GLACIER
1975'
Fortuna Bay
Second Milestone
2742'
Macaroni penguin colony (50,000)
First Milestone
Hercules Bay
Turpie Rock
Humpback Rocks
Cape Saunders
Leith whaling station
Framnæs Pt.
Black Rocks
Harbour Pt.
Stromness Bay
Grass Is.
Stromness whaling station
Tönsberg Pt.
Pt. Purvis
Busen Pt.
Jumbo Cove
Jason Is.
KÖNIG GLACIER
2826
Kelp Pt.
Justa Peak 1618'
Right whale sighted near Jason Is.
Husvick whaling station
Kanin Pt.
3156'
2444
Parsons Peak 1168'
Allen Bay
Jason Peak 2217'
Tor Point
Larsen Pt.
Dog Tooth Pass
2096'
Olsen Valley
Jason Harbour
Cumberland Bay
Admiralty Peak 3100'
Gulbrandsen Lake
Enten Bay
from Maiviken and Grytviken
NEUMAYER GLACIER
1806'
Cumberland West Bay
Hut
Carlita Bay

Legend:
——— Curlew
·········· Ski and hike (Winter and Summer)

STROMNESS BAY

The journey to Leith, one of three abandoned whaling stations in Stromness Bay, was just 20 miles but a miserable, slow plug into short, tumbling seas and against a current. The landmarks passed slowly. Grytviken disappeared and then so did the three-story Shackleton House, which is the soldiers' barracks. We could look up to the white cross erected in 1922 in Sir Ernest Shackleton's memory. At last we rounded Sappho Point and then started a long, discouraging beat across the bay, the wind forcing us to point *Curlew*'s bows far from Larsen Point and Jason Island where we wanted to go. But then suddenly a black-and-white

*Previous spread: One of the largest king penguin colonies on South Georgia is at Salisbury Plain in the Bay of Isles. Most of these thousands of birds have eggs, which they incubate on their feet, held in place by a fold of skin. There are little groups of kings all around South Georgia's coast as well as many colonies of the smaller gentoo penguin (**opposite**). This group gathers around the derelict rowboats at Leith whaling station in Stromness Bay.*

missile exploded out of the wave face in front of us: a bull killer whale with his magnificent 6-foot-high dorsal fin trailing foam. "You see, if we had a motor and were just steaming for Husvik, we would never have seen that," Tim marveled. The fin continued away from us at high speed emitting an almost lethal sense of purpose.

Perhaps the knowledge that Jérôme and his crew had been attacked by a killer whale heightened our imagination. The boat had been a modern, wooden racing yacht called *Guia* and sank within a few minutes of the attack leaving the men scrambling into a life raft. Happily they were picked up less than twenty-four hours later and the drama took place in the warm seas near the equator in the Atlantic. Jérôme wondered if the sailing yacht hadn't represented a whale in some way, inciting the killer whale to ram at great speed with its reinforced skull into the forward sections in just the same way as it might have dealt a lethal blow to the throat of a large whale.

Three inshore 10-foot-high rocks acted as milestones over the next stage and we took bearings to be sure to avoid the isolated Discovery Rock which broke furiously with a great aquamarine crest. Then the breeze dropped right away leaving *Curlew* wallowing in a lumpy leftover sea that gradually became smoother as we spent the next few hours rowing the remaining 4 miles across Stromness Bay and into Leith Harbour. "You see, if we had a motor we'd be safely anchored by now," I ragged Tim.

It was just after nightfall. The shrieks and roars, howls and gurgles echoing back at us from the sheer hillsides were almost more than we could take. It was like some Dantean nightmare with all the monsters of the underworld combining to scare us away. By daylight they would resolve into elephant and fur seals, but for strangers to the place it was quite unnerving. We groped our way to anchor amidst the kelp, with the silhouettes of a whale catcher mast and cranes, tanks, and derelict buildings of Leith whaling station not detracting at all from the otherworldliness.

WE SPENT OUR TIME EXPLORING THE WHALING STATION for artifacts and quality timber for use at Grytviken. Leith Harbour used to belong to the British company Salvesens of Leith. Besides being used for local whaling it was also the transit base for many of the pelagic whalers who did their dastardly deeds farther south. Being larger and away from the beaten track at Grytviken, it still has enormous stocks of raw materials, although most of the more easily removed and desirable smaller items have gone.

Between forays around the derelict buildings, old stores, and accommodation blocks we were entertained everywhere by the fur seal pups who, no longer being suckled by their mothers, were gathering in playful groups. The inner harbor was like a swimming pool for them and they played with the same energy that all youngsters have in that situation. A sturdy round log that spun and revolved in the water was the choice plaything. The young seals would attempt to sit on it and then be spun off left and right, only to leap back on again upsetting the new "king on the mountain."

Tim found that a shrill whistle from him would bring the entire mob of fifty or more to immediate attention, little whiskery faces turned toward him while agile bodies trod water and they all bunched up close to *Curlew*. Then a clap of his hands and they would lunge away, scattering as though afraid of the big bad wolf. Another whistle and again they would

Curlew *waits in Hercules Bay while we take some of the British Antarctic Survey people from the summer research station at Husvik for a change of scene. We have forged close friendships with the BAS scientists, many of whom return summer after summer to research elephant seals, king penguins, and other wildlife.*

zero in on him simultaneously and earnestly watch for the hand-clapping signal to wheel away. Tim tired of this game long before they did, but it was quite amazing while it lasted.

We walked a mile or so south around the coast and across the hills to Stromness, the second of the whaling stations within Stromness Bay. It is not as large and was eventually taken over by

Salvesens of Leith for major refit work on its vessels. There are still massive amounts of heavy machinery and spare parts here.

Stromness is mostly remembered as the whaling station at which Sir Ernest Shackleton and his companions arrived after their epic crossing of the island to get help to rescue the rest of their men. The manager's villa where they were first given baths and food is still standing although severely decayed and it is easy to imagine the three scarecrows first being shunned by the shocked whalers for their appalling state and then being honored and respected when it became obvious who they were, where they had come from, and

what they had just done. We walked back to Leith with our heads full of thoughts of Shackleton's adventures.

Curlew was quite literally bulging at the seams with timber and trophies for the museum when a week later we sailed to Husvik at the head of Stromness Bay. Although it looks uncomfortably exposed to the open sea, there are so many reefs and matted patches of kelp to damp down the waves that we have found it to be quite a safe harbor. This is where the smallest whaling station lies, which the British Antarctic Survey people use as their summer field base. They were busy packing up, ready to be taken out by the royal research ship *Bransfield*, but found time to share coffee and tell us about the work they had been doing over the past two or three seasons.

Elephant seals and king penguins were the major studies and the most interesting to us,

Above: *We wave goodbye to BAS personnel.*
Opposite: *The* Royal Research Ship Bransfield *makes her last call to carry BAS scientists back to England before the onset of winter.* Curlew *is anchored off the old jetty at Husvik.*

but there had also been a beetle lady, a pond man, and marine biologists who had come for a month or so at varying stages of the summer so that up to ten men and women had been staying in the old manager's villa.

Now at the end of the season there were only four men left and nearly all of their equipment and samples were boxed up ready for departure the next day. The big red ship was anchored far out in the bay and we helped to load everything onto carts that traveled on railway tracks along the ramshackle old jetty to the launches that were collecting the cargo. We had a brief meeting with a dozen or more bearded scientists and assistants from the

*Above: "Eco-tourists" come from the other ends of the earth to see the spectacle of king penguins at St. Andrews Bay. Here wild animals are unafraid of humans. **Opposite:** A mother king tends to her chick, nicknamed "oakum boys" by the island's nineteenth-century sealers because their downy brown suits resemble the teased-out hemp used in those days for caulking ships.*

bases farther south who were already on the ship and heading home. They all came ashore to help with the cargo handling, no matter how senior, and then headed off purposefully to catch a glimpse of South Georgia, fanning out for a mile or two in every direction.

This was the beginning of our friendship with many of the BAS people, especially those who came back year after year.

Although it was lovely to sail to Husvik in the winter, when it was deserted, it was always especially good to spend time in summer with whoever was inhabiting the little white house at the edge of the bay. They were always so keen and enthusiastic and we had an excellent time taking them sailing and sharing a few meals while picking their brains for insights into the island's wildlife.

EVERY MID-WINTER WE SAIL TO HUSVIK to count the king penguins and their chicks for Olof, one of the BAS scientists. The adult birds, over 3 feet tall and averaging 26 pounds, are surely the loveliest, definitely the most elegant, of all the penguins. The small colony of about fifty pairs is ideal for close research; Olof could identify every adult by a numbered flipper band and the chicks by a numbered spot he used to glue on their backs. If all goes well the kings stay faithful to one mate. The major part of the study took four years, although information still trickles in. In the summer of 1996-97 one of Olof's banded birds turned up in the Falkland Islands.

Another of our tasks has been to remove the transponders that are glued onto the backs of some of the adult kings to record information on their dives. They travel at almost 8 miles an hour and frequently dive to about 160 feet for about 8 minutes, but a dive to almost 1,000 feet has been recorded. The king penguin makes approximately 865 dives per foraging trip of about a week to ten days in summer. And the distance traveled is up to 350 miles, generally north to the edge of the polar front in summer, farther to the west in winter. This latest information on their early winter journeys has come from the transponders Tim took from two Husvik birds.

Unlike the chicks of other penguins, who leave at the end of summer, king chicks stay at their colonies until the following spring. The youngsters have to survive much colder condi-

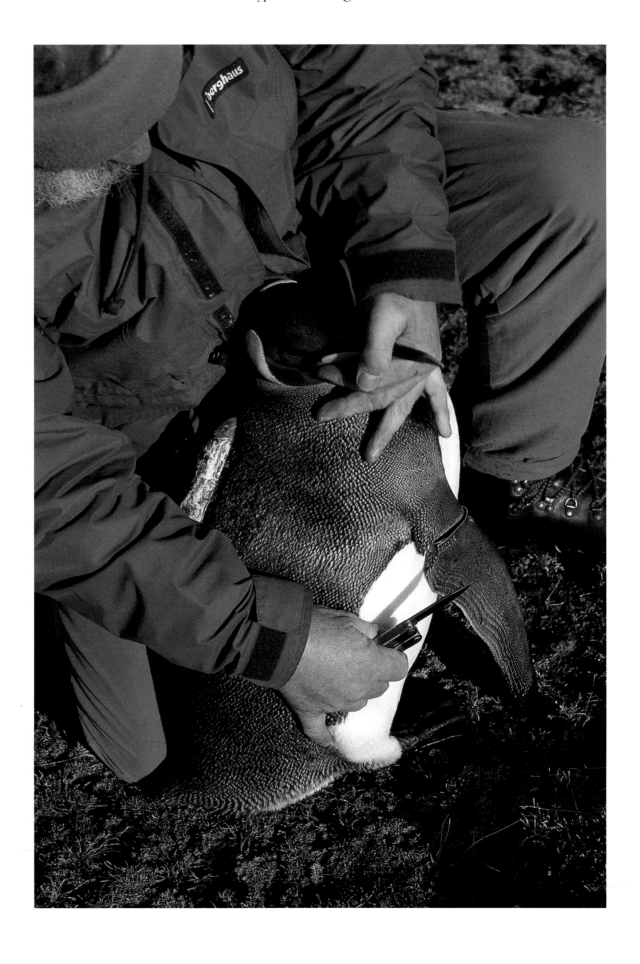

tions on land than they would need to at sea, where the temperature is not much below freezing. In April, still in their brown, downy coats, they huddle together in nurseries hungrily awaiting the adults' return to feed them whenever they have found enough food — often only once a week or so and even less during the middle part of the winter when the chicks are virtually fasting for a couple of months and slowly losing the vital weight they need to survive. By spring they may well have lost half the body mass that they reached in late summer, and often we find a fresh carcass providing a feast for the giant petrels to testify to the failures.

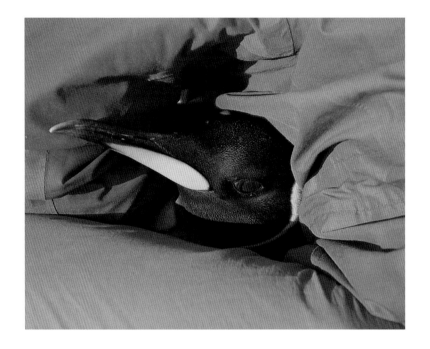

Meanwhile the "oakum boys" (the name given to them by the sealers, who likened their fuzzy coats to the teased-out hemp that was used in those days for caulking ships) always seem to have a phalanx of adults shepherding them solicitously into the most sheltered spots for the prevailing wind conditions.

King penguins walk slowly and deliberately, and we learned to differentiate them from the smaller penguins at a distance because they generally hold their flippers down by their sides while the others walk with them spread out for balance. They nearly always breed close to a river and it is relatively easy to locate colonies this way. When molting they prefer to stand on the cool surface of any remaining patch of snow and will go to great lengths to reach it, where they are easy to pick out against the white background.

The glorious gold of the king penguin's ear patches and bib radiates like sunshine even on the darkest of days. A colony with eggs, which they keep atop their large black feet and tucked under a soft, downy brood pouch, all face the same direction and look like a field of sunflowers amidst the trodden earth. Their backs are not black but a steely blue. It is hard to pick out the details of the soft brown eyes set into a jet black head. Right at the end of the

Tim removes a transponder from the back of an adult king at the Husvik colony. The devices have shown that kings frequently dive to 160 feet and make about 865 dives per foraging trip of a week to ten days in summer. The distance traveled on such a trip is up to 350 miles, generally north to the edge of the polar front in summer, farther west in winter.

rose-colored plate that adorns the rapier-sharp bill we have spotted an almost iridescent blue flash in a few, select birds — maybe at the peak of their breeding plumage.

While at Husvik we make the best of our time to walk or ski into the hinterland. The Olsen Valley is where the kings live, at the mouth of the Olsen River. If we follow the river up and then descend again we reach Carlita Bay on Cumberland Bay West, with stunning views of the Neumayer glacier and the Three Brothers mountains. The whalers called these Tom, Dick, and Harry — but we still haven't discovered which is which.

Inland from the South Valley at Husvik there is a particularly magical place. Gulbrandsen Lake used to be several hundred feet deep and is still substantial in summer when it is full of bergy bits broken off a minor snout of the Neumayer glacier. Later in the year something, and it is not clear what, causes it to empty — all of a sudden, like a giant's bathtub, in a matter of days. Then all the bergy bits are stranded on the black shale lake bed and get sculpted by the wind into amazing shapes of beautiful colors. When the snows come we can ski between these contoured ice castles and feel as though we have left our planet for some Krypton-like wonderland.

Apart from elephant seals, Husvik does not have large numbers of wildlife, although there is a fair representation of quite a lot of different species, which is why the BAS values it. But it is an especially good place for reindeer.

These magnificent animals, known as caribou in North America, are found anywhere around Stromness Bay, where the initial small herd of animals was brought in from Norway by the whalers in 1912 for sport and meat. There are now perhaps a thousand after a succession of good years. They do not congregate in one giant herd but separate into groups:

A late summer visit to Gulbrandsen Lake, a magical landscape inland from the South Valley at Husvik. Here some years, we know not why, the lake suddenly loses its water, leaving bergy bits from the Neumayer glacier stranded on the black shale lake bed.

herds of 100 or more in late autumn and small groups (a stag with a harem of 8 or 12) during the rutt in March. Their range extends from the Fortuna glacier in the north to the Neumayer glacier in the south.

There are also another thousand or so reindeer on the Barff Peninsula to the southeastern side of Cumberland Bay East, who are the descendants of ten animals introduced in 1911. They extend all the way down the coast to Royal Bay, their range curtailed only by impassable glaciers. As the glaciers recede — they are all doing so now at an alarming rate, presumably because of global warming — the reindeer may eventually be able to cross the moraines and extend their territory, dramatically eradicating the burnet and any lichens within reach. They occasionally interfere with penguins and other breeding birds, too, if something causes a herd to gallop off in their direction.

We were once skiing between Husvik and Stromness when a herd approached us from upwind at full gallop. They scarcely wavered to split on either side of us and went thundering past with huge hooves churning up the snow like a miniature blizzard. In winter it doesn't matter, but in summer a giant petrel's nest or a colony of penguins wouldn't stand much of a chance.

Ash, a New Zealander who looked after the maintenance of the BAS station and the safety of its personnel in the field, warned us that stags in rut could be the most dangerous animals we would meet in South Georgia and advised us not to approach them too closely. Chiefly in March and April, they seem to lose all fear and stand their ground ready to chase off any intruder. At this time their antlers are magnificent, especially if there has been good grazing. In fact, you can tell what kind of year it has been by the size of the antlers. By winter the stags have cast their antlers, and it can get confusing (to humans, anyway) because the female reindeer do have relatively small antlers (the only deer species where this is

the case) and retain them all through the winter. It is obvious that Santa borrows Rudolph and the rest of his sleigh-pulling animals from the South Georgian herds — because Scandinavian reindeer have all cast their antlers before Christmas!

Since Chernobyl's ghastly cloud penetrated the mosses and reindeer fodder of the Northern Hemisphere, the southern herds have taken on increasing scientific value. It is also interesting to see a species adapt to an environment very different from its natural one. An obvious example is that they had to change from breeding in the northern spring to the spring of the Southern Hemisphere — fully six months later. It must have been very hard surviving during the first few years when their heavy coats would molt in the wrong season and their calves would be born at the beginning of winter. Yet they did survive and adapt so that there are arguments both for and against letting them remain in South Georgia.

*Opposite: A lone reindeer stag near Husvik in autumn. Reindeer, or caribou, were imported to South Georgia by Norwegian whalers in 1911 for sport and meat. Today there are up to 2,000 animals on the island, many near Husvik. **Above:** Pauline watched, spellbound, as this fur seal gave birth. The mother picked up the pup in her mouth as soon as it was born.*

ASH, TIM, AND I DECIDED TO WALK TO STROMNESS where Tim was to make a survey of wood to be shipped to Grytviken to repair the church roof. But Ash pointed out a female fur seal coming up onto the beach that he could see was heavily pregnant. Most of the pups had already been born during the first week of December so I opted to stay and watch in the hope that she would give birth. Nobody ever seems to see this happen unless they are either very lucky or working continuously among fur seals.

Four very pleasant, indolent hours later I was rewarded with a breach birth — not that unusual. But it was extraordinary to see the female lying down on her back and apparently sprouting an extra pair of flippers. The pup popped out in a matter of seconds and immediately made fur seal pup noises — not unlike a gruff lamb. Then the mother wailed in the peculiar and unique call, her own identifiable voice, that would herald her return with milk every few days for the next four months. Mucous membranes fell away and she picked up the pup in her mouth just like a dog, presumably having to be extra careful with her ferocious self-sharpening teeth. She ran around with her offspring, putting it down and then picking it up again and wailing whenever she didn't have her mouth full. I thought the pup might get quite dizzy but its eyes opened immediately and its little red mouth showed a full complement of pearly sharp teeth. It started to scratch as naturally as though it had been scratching all its life. Tiny black claws emerged from halfway down its flippers, unlike the "true" seals whose flippers terminate with almost human nails. Fur seals, like sea lions and walruses, are "eared" seals and differ in many ways from the true seals, which are much less mobile on land.

When Tim and Ash came back I must have looked like the cat that had got the cream and they both humored me and stayed a while longer to admire such a special little pup. There may be nearly a million pups born in the island every year but this was definitely a one-in-a-million for me.

The BAS has pulled out of Husvik now, their various projects completed. We hope they will come back in a few years but in the meantime we still visit the old field station, unbolt the door, and sit by the window watching the seals and penguins and remembering the various friends we made over four summers and the good times we all shared.

A giant petrel soars over a lone caribou stag near Husvik. The animals do not congregate in one giant herd but break into groups: herds of 100 or more in late autumn and small groups (a stag with a harem of 8 or 12) during the rutt in March. Their range in this region of South Georgia extends from the Fortuna glacier in the north to the Neumayer glacier in the south.

CHAPTER VI

SHACKLETON'S SHADOW

May 19, 1993

*C*urlew HAD BEGUN TO SURGE a little and the mooring lines were creaking. It was still dark when Tim slid out of our bunk, awakened by the abrasive and insistent grating of ice. Soon I could hear him driving a series of holes around the boat with a sharp boathook and fragmenting the edges of the pancake ice close to *Curlew*, which cushioned her hull from the effects of the big plates of 2-inch-thick ice.

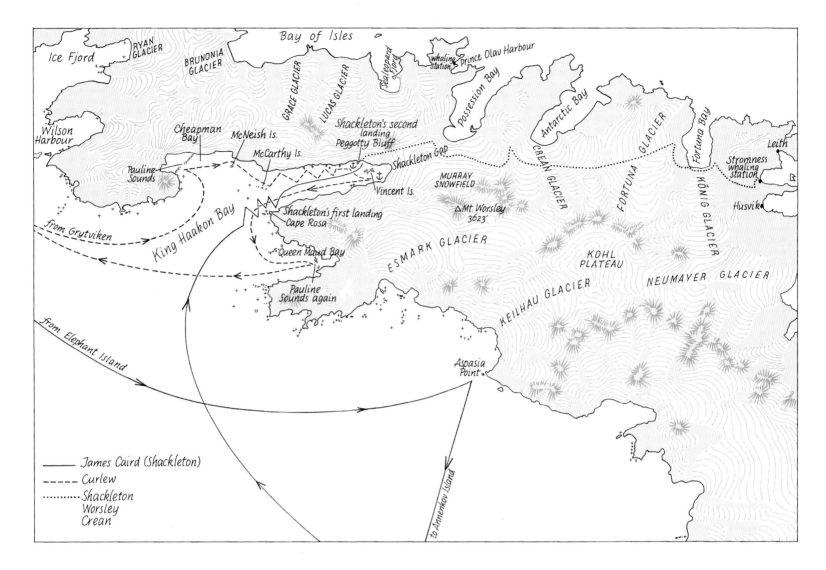

SHACKLETON'S
AND *CURLEW*'S
ROUTES

Such a rude awakening; I suppressed the urge to doze and left the warm bunk too. Putting on the cabin heater and priming the stove for tea, I glanced at the thermometer — minus 8 degrees Celsius (18 degrees Fahrenheit) — and shot rapidly back under the quilt.

The previous day had been spent hiking on the lower slopes of the mountains; the air was very cold but our bodies were warm with the exertion of crossing Glacier Col to watch fresh snow avalanche off Sugartop Mountain. We had gone to bed with Jupiter so clear that we could see its ring of moons through our ship's binoculars. But now awakening with Venus veiled in cirrus, combined with the surging, told us that the wind would not be long in coming.

Previous spread: Curlew is dwarfed by the jagged mountains and massive unnamed glacier at the head of King Haakon Bay, scene of Sir Ernest Shackleton's 1916 landing in the 22-foot-long James Caird, *after an 800-mile passage.*

We nursed our steaming mugs and I noticed the date on my watch. "They set off today." No need for Tim to ask who. The spirits of three men loom very large in South Georgia and one lies buried here, a few hundred yards from *Curlew*'s berth, in the Grytviken cemetery — Sir Ernest Shackleton, Antarctic explorer and expedition leader extraordinaire.

On this day, almost eighty years earlier, Shackleton had set off from the far side of this island to cross the icecaps and mountain ranges, hitherto considered impassable, to reach Stromness whaling station and raise help. With him were Captain Frank Worsley of New Zealand, a forty-four-year-old veteran of square rigged ships, and big, strong, second mate Tom Crean, an Irishman who had already proved his worth with two Scott expeditions. They left three men behind on that forbidding coast and the remainder of the expedition, twenty-two men, marooned on remote Elephant Island, 800 miles to the southwest across the Scotia Sea. That 800 hard-earned miles of frigid, fiercesome, gale-swept Southern Ocean had been overcome by a mere ordinary ship's whaler, a cockleshell 22 feet 6 inches long, with a name that has become legendary: *James Caird.*

No snuggling in the fo'c'sle under warm quilts for these men, but struggling out of reindeer-skin sleeping bags, long denuded of hair by the constant saltwater soakings and hard usage. No mugs of tea while they pulled on warm, dry, synthetic polarwear suits by the glow of a diesel heater. But at 2 a.m. they endeavored to put life back into stiff limbs as they crawled out from the crowded shelter of little upturned *James Caird* and an elephant seal blubber fire. Only the hiss of the Primus stove is a link back between us. In 1916, their drama reached a crescendo under a full moon; in 1993 the moon had fallen a little earlier in the month, but we had recognized it and called it Shackleton's moon.

The 550-ton barkentine-rigged *Endurance* had finally submitted to the ice, crushed after an immense struggle of nearly a year, on November 21, 1915. Her position was 68 degrees South in the Weddell Sea and some 240 miles east of the nearest icebound coast of Antarctica. The twenty-eight men had then spent five months living on ice floes, with their tents and three boats. The floes began to jostle, fracture, and fragment as they were carried north to warmer seas. Against all odds the three overloaded boats, the smallest with a freeboard of only 17 inches, made a six-day journey to Elephant Island in the South Shetland group. Their crews had very little sleep as they fought gales and subzero temperatures, often bailing for their lives.

Then Shackleton chose five men to accompany him on the most hazardous stage — he later said, "The ocean south of Cape Horn in the middle of May is known to be the most tempestuous, storm-swept area of water in the world. . .the tale of the next sixteen days is one of supreme strife amid heaving waters."

In fact ten of those days saw gale-force winds with frequent swampings; at one point the boat was coated with 15 inches of ice which had to be chipped off. No one had oilskins or seaboots, while even below the makeshift canvas decks there was little respite. The sleeping bags were wet or frozen, there was no sitting headroom, and a major effort was required from at least three men to produce hot food from the Primus.

Before we could even place South Georgia accurately on a map we were aware of this incredible small-boat journey — probably the greatest ever — and when we had decided to spend our first year on the island it was partly to see the spiritual places where Cook, Weddell, and then Shackleton had walked. And so it came about that on another early morning, this time the following midsummer, *Curlew* spread her synthetic wings to a sun-warmed breeze and traveled gently to the west.

Past the whaling stations of Leith, Stromness, and Husvik; past Possession Bay where Captain Cook had first landed in 1775 and fired his three-volley salute to "Take Possession

in his Britannic Majesty's Name and His Heirs for ever"; through an uncharacteristically benign Bird Sound amid great, grounded icebergs and gliding albatrosses. On the southwestern coast there are few good anchorages, so we made the most of Undine Harbour, where Captain Weddell had sheltered in 1823, for a quiet night.

The next morning the weather was still amazingly fair, the barometer was steady, and the motivation was strong. "We'll try it," said Tim, tongue firmly in cheek, echoing the words of Shackleton, who used this phrase whenever faced by daunting challenges.

The moderate southwesterly breeze was perfect — it would have been dangerous from that direction in a gale pushing the little boat onto the coast, but there was nothing to worry

*Above: We seek a safe anchorage in Cheapman Bay, but Pauline cannot find enough depth for us beyond the moraine barrier and and into shelter. **Opposite:** A bergy bit grounded on the moraine bar at Cheapman Bay — settling place for kelp gulls.*

about on a day as brilliant as this. When Shackleton and his men made their landfall in *James Caird* after fourteen days, they had been forced by a hard gale to heave-to overnight. On the next day Shackleton wrote, "By noon the gale had risen to hurricane force, hauled to the southwest and was driving us, harder than ever, straight for that ironbound coast. As we

drove inshore it seemed that only three or four of the giant, deep-sea swells separated us from the cliffs of destruction — the coast of death."

There were no soundings on our 1988 chart from about 10 miles offshore. At best there was an occasional + (indicating a reef) with "PA" (position approximate) or "PD" (position doubtful) or even "ED" (existence doubtful) to confuse the issue. Captain Worsley wrote that "sudden great spouts of white and terrific roaring combers showed where the battle raged between the wild westerly swell and uncharted reefs off the coast." *Curlew*, too, avoided three of these unmarked dangers. Since then the British Hydrographic Office has verified our discoveries and the admiralty charts have been amended.

Toward afternoon we sighted Annenkov Island, illusive and magical, seldom visited by humans. It had nearly defeated the *James Caird*, as noted by Captain Worsley: "The mountain peak of Annenkov Island loomed menacingly close on the lee bow. . .at one time we were almost in the yeasty backwash of the surf." But for *Curlew* the barometer needle was motionless and time likewise seemed to stand still. The coastline had begun to rise ever more dramatically; glaciers and icecaps became the dominant feature with many icebergs grounded or drifting along our track.

Cirrus, faint wisps of high cloud in the western sky. No words, but we both knew the

Above: Out comes the oar as we enter King Haakon Bay. With the barometer dropping we urge Curlew *on toward an anchorage for the night.* **Opposite:** *Looking out to sea with Cape Rosa in the distance. Three glaciers tumble to the shore, but Shackleton counted a total of twelve that spilled into King Haakon Bay.*

needle had moved a hair's breadth down. The wind fell light, the topsail and biggest jib went up, and a rubber shock absorber took the roll and snatch from the heavy boom. We turned and ran downwind slowly toward the bight into which King Haakon Bay flows. *Curlew* drifted on toward Cheapman Bay, a large, glacially carved harbor with a moraine barrier across its entrance marked by kelp and one large rock. Tim hove *Curlew* to, bringing her to a virtual halt, while I took the leadline off in the dinghy to sound the entrance, feeling vulnerable and dwarfed by the towering mountains and tumbling glaciers. There was just enough water through a very narrow channel in the kelp but beyond it the dinghy was lifted

Peggotty Bluff. Here Shackleton brought the James Caird *ashore, where she would be sheltered from the prevailing winds. The boat was then upturned so that the six men could live underneath her in the manner of Charles Dickens's Peggotty in* David Copperfield.

suddenly on a steep wave, almost a breaker. The deepest sounding was a disappointing 5 feet, *Curlew* having a draft of over 6 feet.

This was a setback, as the nearest anchorage was now at the head of King Haakon Bay, 10 miles away. The light was fading after an increasingly spectacular sunset and the breeze had almost completely ceased. On board the barometer had dropped radically. "Oh, fools rush in," we thought, looking uneasily at the blank chart with its random smattering of +s. But the *Antarctic Pilot* came to the rescue again with a concise description of a passage north of McNeish Island, north of McCarthy Islands, and with relatively few big-ship dangers beyond.

In what we jokingly refer to as "motor-sailing mode," Tim used the 14-foot oar while I towed *Curlew* along with the dinghy. The anchor was hooked over the little boat's stern with a length of chain absorbing the shocks and jerks of individual oar strokes.

In the dusk we slopped past McNeish Island. McNeish was the carpenter aboard *Endurance*, a "splendid shipwright, over fifty years of age and not altogether fit but [he] had a good knowledge of sailing boats and was very quick." When the *James Caird* arrived at King Haakons he was described as "all in" and probably wouldn't have lasted another twenty-four hours. We gave thanks to McNeish for its lee and steadying influence, the sails began to draw again fitfully, and it was time to take a break from rowing and make a cuppa.

This reminded us of the men in the boat whose water supply had been tainted so they hadn't had a drink for several days. Thirst had become their greatest enemy after their miraculous escape from the lee shore. They, too, had been rowing into King Haakon, but at the end of their sixteenth day at sea a strong easterly headwind had sprung up suddenly to compound their difficulties.

Easterly! Cat's-paws ruffled the water around *Curlew*. McCarthy Islands gave us still more lee from the swell and rose in steep outcrops silhouetted against the last red light in the sky. Able seaman Timothy McCarthy was "a simple, honest, brave, smiling, golden-hearted, merchant service Jack," said Worsley. "We, his shipmates, who truly learned his worth in that boat journey, are proud of his memory." Six months after his rescue he went down with his ship in World War I, "fighting his gun to the last."

Cape Rosa, too, was outlined against that ominous sky. Here the men had found a narrow channel through the surf, landed the boat, and fallen to their knees in the sweet water of a little stream. They discovered a cave, really just a shallow indentation in the rock face, where six bodies could at long last lie stretched on the solid earth. A screen of boat sails was slung behind a line of 10- to 15-foot-long icicles.

But *Curlew* was not yet at rest. It had started to snow and we were busy reducing the amount of sail in anticipation of a rising wind. There was no light left, but with eyes straining through snow goggles, we could see the glaciers and the considerable amount of ice and snow aloft. This helped to delineate the long sound as *Curlew* crisscrossed it, making her progress by counting the glaciers passed. A stream of glacial ice tossed in the inky water ahead. Tack. A dark and growing outline stood out against the white. It was Peggotty Bluff, Shackleton's second camp, so called because the faithful *James Caird* was upturned here, surrounded with rocks and thatched all around with tussock to resemble Charles Dickens's original creation from David Copperfield.

The ship's anchorage described in the *Pilot* was exposed to the winds with a depth of over 140 feet; in the dark we dared not approach the third group of islands, Vincent, for shelter, as there were yet more +s surrounding them on the chart for quite a distance. But with the strong easterly now howling down from the icecap, Peggotty Bluff provided just the shelter needed and *Curlew* wriggled her way in cautiously until the leadline found 10 fathoms — 60 feet. We grappled with the staysail in gale-force gusts and then dropped the anchor with all of its chain.

THE BAROMETER PLUMMETED ALL NIGHT, the fastest fall we'd seen all summer. The veering gale began to give us a rough motion as the sea found its way between Peggotty Bluff and Vincent Islands, but with the other anchors ready to drop, *Curlew* dipped to it in relative comfort. By dawn there was a lull and enough time to retrieve the well-buried, mud-covered anchor and sail around to the far side of Vincent Islands. We anchored as close to the kelp line as we dared, laying out two other anchors to cover all possible wind directions.

Sure enough, after the glass had bottomed out, the wind came screaming in from the west, southwest, a 180-degree switch but the Vincent Islands were there to give us shelter. Vincent was another able seaman, a North Sea fisherman before he sailed with *Endurance*, who could scarcely have expected such a memorial.

All the glacial ice that had been streaming out of King Haakon Bay during the easterly winds was now being driven back toward *Curlew*. So we had another sleepless and traumatic night wearing headlights and taking it in turns to fend off the bigger pieces as they homed in on us. It was physically exhausting to lunge at each one with the sharp point of the

Curlew dwarfed, just as the James Caird *must have been, by the austere coastline at King Haakon Bay. These cliffs rise sharply from the sea, culminating in 3,998-foot Mount Cunningham.*

boathook and then try to deflect the heavy, dingy-sized lumps before they could batter and bruise our vulnerable hull.

By dawn, though, the anchorage was clear. Slightly fuzzy from our broken nights, we sat in the cockpit to admire the awesome views. To quote again from Shackleton, "The long bay had been a magnificent sight, even to eyes that had dwelt on grandeur long enough and were hungry for the simple, familiar things of everyday life. Its green-blue waters were being beaten into a fury by the northwesterly gale. The mountains, stern peaks that dared the stars, peered through the mists and between them huge glaciers poured down from the great icy slopes and fields that lay behind. We counted twelve glaciers and heard every few minutes the reverberating roar caused by masses of ice calving from the parent streams."

Above us an unnamed mountain rose sheer to 2,500 feet with higher peaks close behind. To the southeast, a towering, chaotic jumble of blue ice overflowed into the bay and, between the two, an overhanging white glacier cascaded tons of brash hundreds of feet into an icy heap beneath. To the northeast the wispy clouds were clearing over Shackleton Gap itself, a smooth, almost inviting glacier that swoops unhindered across the north of the island into Possession Bay.

If the whaling stations had lain in this direction, Shackleton's task would have seemed feasible. As it was, the three exhausted, bone-weary, and ill-equipped men had to cross not only this great ice sheet but then the four mountain ridges that lay athwart the island between them and Stromness Bay.

With no map of the island — for one didn't exist — and a very rough piece of chart of the coast, Shackleton, Worsley, and Crean had to retrace their steps several times. They made three attempts on one ridge alone, each arduous climb meeting with precipices on the other side. With only a short length of rope, a cut-down ship's adze, and 2-inch brass nails through the soles of their worn-out boots for grip, they marched continuously for nearly thirty-six hours until they overlooked Stromness Bay. From there they made a final and difficult descent, through a bone-chilling waterfall, to the whaling station. Here they presented such a fearful sight that the first few men who saw them turned away in horror.

While the weather was fair we took the dinghy ashore to top up with water. Both Shackleton and Worsley had written about an 8-foot-high mound of wreckage "piled in utter

*Curlew anchored at the head of King Haakon Bay near Shackleton Gap,
a low receding glacier that crosses to the north side of the island. Yet far higher mountains
and more treacherous glaciers lay in Shackleton's path to Stromness whaling station and rescue.*

confusion" and in which lay "beautifully carved figureheads, well-turned teak stanchions with brass caps, handrails clothed in canvas coachwhipping finished off with Turk's heads, cabin doors, broken skylights, teak scuttles, binnacle stands, boat skids, gratings, headboards, barricoes, oars and harness casks." We found only a portion of old pinrail, with holes for the belaying pins and cutouts for the rigging, and a spar with a squared-off heel.

Peggotty Bluff is a lovely, mossy, tussock-covered hill, a good lee against the persistent winds. It was quite wonderful to imagine the sight that greeted the castaways McCarthy, McNeish, and Vincent as the whaler *Samson* came steaming to the rescue with Captain Worsley aboard. He was now so well shaved, washed, and clothed that his companions of nearly two years failed to recognize him.

James Caird was lifted reverently on board and eventually returned to Britain where she was exhibited; she is now kept carefully at the Dulwich College in London.

Meanwhile, Shackleton had been offered the whaler *Southern Sky* to rescue the Elephant Island party. But it took four attempts with four different ships before he, Worsley, and Crean, who remained with him, were able to find a relatively ice-free time and the island could be approached safely and all twenty-two men rescued.

But it is the spirit of the six men on the narrowest of dividing lines between success and failure, life and death, that pervades King Haakon Bay. For us aboard *Curlew* it was the highlight of our summer; pure adventure. In Shackleton's words: "high adventure, strenuous days, lonely nights, unique experiences."

SOME YEARS LATER Tim was invited to a Royal Geographical Society lecture and dinner. When he arrived in London he was laden down with a 75-liter backpack and incongruously still wearing his South Georgia boots. Unfortunately, this intrepid navigator got a bit lost and panicky in the concrete wastelands of the city, kept asking people for directions, and went around in circles while the traffic ground remorselessly past. Dusk was coming on until there were only a few minutes left before he was due at the talk. Suddenly he became aware of a statue towering above him. He looked up and thought, "Oh, I know you." It was Sir Ernest, and lo and behold there was the imposing facade of the building. Tim slid in via the back door and Shackleton had rescued yet another traveler when all had seemed lost . . . .

Shackleton's gravestone at Grytviken cemetery is visited by a group of molting king penguins. The great explorer died aboard Quest *while anchored in King Edward Cove in 1922.*

CHAPTER VII

The ROUGH
with the SMOOTH

June-September (Winter) 1993

BEFORE WE COULD SAFELY CONSIDER CRUISING in the winter we had to learn to ski. With several feet of snow even at sea level this was the only way to move around. It would quickly become almost impossible to walk between *Curlew* and the museum as the drifts banked up above the windows and in some cases up to the roofs.

At first we taught ourselves and at least achieved a certain degree of balance if nothing elegant. Then to our delight the Royal Marine mountain leader, the instructor at the garrison, asked us if we'd like to join his arctic survival course and we jumped at the chance.

It opened up a whole new magical world so that now as each summer progresses we long for the first major snowfall. Then, in April or May, the island becomes as beautiful as a young bride in white lace and we relish the speed and ease with which parts of the winter island can be traversed. Conversely, as the spring thaws come in October we become nostalgic and then rapidly uninspired when the ski boots have to be exchanged for walking boots and we feel like birds with clipped wings. In fact, downright pedestrian.

The soldiers lent us wooden skis without metal edges — primitive things that had long since disappeared from anywhere except museums and the South Georgia garrison. But if we could manage with those here, we could manage anywhere. So we struggled to plow to a stop and to maneuver on steeper slopes without our heavy packs tipping us and sending us into a crumpled heap some undignified distance below. Cross-country army skis are designed to go uphill too, and so we learned to herringbone or sidestep for what felt like miles to our aching thighs. The mountain leader took pity on us and offered "skins" — velvety stick-ons that give good grip going uphill and make things a lot easier in some conditions.

As three winters passed we began to get quite proficient and even to master the graceful art of telemarking, the ability to turn in scything, bowing sweeps, almost kneeling on the skis, and to descend steep slopes of virgin powder with an ease that is astonishing. Now we had progressed to fancier civilian skis with metal edges and three-pin bindings to fit expen-

Previous spread: The eastern corrie of Lyell glacier has recently proved to be a good route for an attempt to climb Mount Sugartop. **Above:** *The Royal Marine mountain leader who taught us to ski is not at all pleased with the conditions as he puts his men and us through our paces.* **Opposite:** *The infantry (Royal Irish Rangers) go ski touring carrying provisions to survive day and night.*

sive boots. The need to ski as a mode of travel had long been overridden by the sheer joy of a new, exhilarating sport.

During the first winter, after we felt sufficiently confident to go cross-country on our own, we sailed to Husvik. First we had to wait for the bay to unfreeze, or rather for the wind

to blow all the ice out to sea. It had been so thick that a foolhardy man could have skied across it to the point. No, we were not that foolhardy. Three minutes in the water and that would be it. I bailed a lot of snow off the decks that we had left there for insulation and Tim let go the protective ice lines that keep any bergy bits and brash ice at bay.

We sailed on a sunny day so that the halyards and lines were not frozen and stiff. The winter days are short with perhaps a maximum of seven hours of usable daylight, assuming clear skies, otherwise more like five in blizzards and bad visibility. It sometimes takes us a couple of hours to get all the anchors up, which further reduces the effective sailing time.

There was little wind but we had a spectacular view of the Allardyce Mountains and so were quite content. Eventually we rowed about 4 miles to Maiviken Cove, happy to be on the move again by any means. To the west of the cove we found a cave that so far had gone unrecorded. There were the remains of a hearth and an old boat spar across the entrance, which had probably supported a sail to keep the worst of the weather out for some hardy band of men in the 1800s — but why had they left it behind? Was their shallop — sealers' small boat — wrecked and, if so, how did they escape? There were also some fragile, tissue-thin, soldered tins in the cave's recesses. Lead-soldered tins had poisoned the Franklin expedition in the Arctic in 1848, so we were, and still are, intrigued by our find.

An evening breeze found *Curlew* trundling across Cumberland Bay West to Jason Harbour, where we paid a visit to the old post hut built in 1911. The 6-mile stretch across the bay

Preparations for a winter cruise. Much as we enjoy ski touring Grytviken's environs, it is impossible for us to resist cruising in Curlew, *even in midwinter. Here Pauline bails snow off* Curlew's *decks (between cruises we let it build up for insulation).*

can frequently cut up rough with a steep choppy sea raised by winds sweeping down the Neumayer glacier and often reaching gale force to bring ice along as well.

This would be a hazardous trip for the rowing boat carrying mail between whaling stations in the summer. After sheltering in the little hut, with its solid-fuel "bogey" stove still there to this day, the intrepid postmen would be off over the ranges for a full day's excursion to reach Husvik. From there the mail would be carried to Stromness and finally Leith.

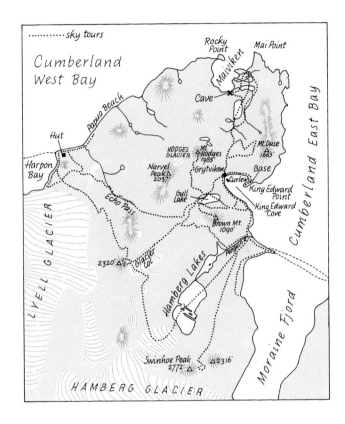

How much easier it was for us to sail directly to Husvik with our seaworthy, decked-in vessel. So the next morning, on a sparkling day, we headed off, bounding out of the bay full of optimism. And for good reason, because shortly after we started Tim spotted a tail — just a tail—held above the water like a glistening ebony fan for minutes at a time. Then as it slipped beneath the water came the double blow that told that it was a right whale.

We had never seen one before and it was thrilling to be so close. *Curlew* sailed toward it gradually but it seemed to have not the slightest concern about us or our ship and we realized how easily the whalers could also have approached. The whale alternated tail-sailing with gentle shallow dives and blows. Then it was easy to see the big rounded back, with no dorsal fin, and the strange, prehistoric-looking

SKI-TOURING

ROUTES

head with its white growths. These callosities, as they are called, are how whale experts can identify individual animals. After an hour we left, knowing we still had some miles to cover to Husvik. The huge black flukes were poised and motionless again and the last thing we saw was a snow petrel, closely circling it and apparently curious as well.

During the first few years that the Norwegians had operated out of Grytviken, they did not have to venture out of Cumberland Bay to catch their prey, yet this was the first "great" whale we had seen after nine months in South Georgia — proof enough of the devastating, ruthless, and avaricious slaughter that swept across these waters for sixty years during which time nearly a quarter of a million whales were killed.

Since then, though, we have seen several more whales and received encouraging reports from ships passing through these waters and the BAS people at Bird Island. Right whales have twice even come to the mouth of King Edward Cove and sperm whales and killers have harassed long-line fishing boats.

When Jérôme first sailed in these and Antarctic Peninsula waters in 1971 he saw virtually no whales. When *Curlew* took us to the peninsula in 1992 there were blows regularly resounding among the icebergs. Rounded blows from fat humpbacks, with their tails flitting on the sea surface like piebald butterflies, tall columns fountaining from long fin whales and short

gasps from little minkies, whose blow begins before they surface. But alas, never the greatest of them all, the giant blue, the largest animal ever to have inhabited the planet and now teetering on the verge of extinction.

As many of the other whale populations begin to recover we hope that they will eventually return to South Georgia's seas and complete this icy Eden.

Just after we had tied up at Husvik a wicked blizzard confined us to the boat in heavy southwesterly winds with violent squalls and what felt like the coldest temperatures yet. We later learned that at the garrison minus 20 degrees Celsius (minus 4 degrees Fahrenheit) had been recorded with winds in excess of 90 knots, producing a wind chill factor of far more than minus 50 degrees Celsius (minus 58 degrees Fahrenheit). Our main sliding hatch froze up completely so that we had to use the forehatch to go out and check the mooring lines, which were frozen into solid blocks where they were tied onto the cleats.

No skiing then; broken sleep at night and light reading by day were all that could be accomplished. Good reception on the radio of the BBC World Service helped to drown out some of the shrieking winds. But somehow the soothing voice of the cricket commentator failed to concentrate our minds on idyllic English pastoral scenes as the winds caught the top of *Curlew's* mast and she heeled subserviently to the relentless Antarctic furies.

Eventually it died down and although the snow was still spuming from the heights above 2,000 feet we felt it safe to go ashore. It was great to be liberated as we waxed the skis with

Opposite: Anchored in Jason Harbour, we stop at the Jason hut. Built by whalers in 1911, until recently it remained well stocked, ready to give shelter to anyone in need.
Above: On our way around to Husvik we came across a placid right whale.

the coldest wax, rated for minus 10 degrees Celsius, clipped our boots into their bindings, and were off — delighting in the swish-swish sound as the wooden skis cut into the icy layers of crisp, fast snow.

Our destination was the king penguin colony at Olsen Valley, where we found thirty-eight chicks. They all looked large and fluffy in their chocolate-colored down coats while forty slim and sleek adults were shepherding them conscientiously. This was a good number and Olof would be very pleased to add it to his records. A leopard seal lay nearby. We hoped it wasn't sleeping off a meal of one of the parent kings. On the beach it posed no threat, but in the water it would be a quite different and very menacing animal.

We had to climb high up the hillside to return without crossing a succession of gorges. The wind became fitful and shadows were crawling across the valley. We paused for a time to absorb the serenity of the wilderness and then turned on our skis and set off downhill, dark insignificant specks amid the grandeur. The solitude was emphasized by the sheer scale of the surroundings and the threadlike tracks, soon to be obliterated by fresh snow, tracing across the hills.

The descent was all too soon over. As our breath steamed in the cold air *Curlew* loomed larger in our sights. We passed into the derelict, eerie whaling station and the twisted sham-bles that were the whalers' legacy to South Georgia. Skis were buckled together and loaded into the dinghy and then lifted aboard and lashed down.

AT THE BEGINNING OF SEPTEMBER we left Grytviken again for Bird Island. It was only 65 miles to sail there directly but it took us the best part of a month. Wicked weather caught up with us in Fortuna Bay and once again we had to get the survival gear out and packed as hurri-cane-force winds driving icy snow threat-ened to pluck *Curlew* from her anchors. We wished we had remembered a shovel to dig a snowhole if we were shipwrecked. This was the only way we just might have survived until better weather would allow us to cross the mountain range to Stromness — as Shackleton had done before and as we had done in fine weather in the summer. But this was entirely dif-ferent and the relentless weather shook our confidence.

Fortuna Bay had proved a frightening place with the high winds and an exposed anchor-age. With another storm imminent we sailed *Curlew* away from these dangers but had to run a gauntlet of strong headwinds and freezing halyards and rigging. In winter the average tem-peratures at sea level in sheltered Grytviken are about minus 4 degrees Celsius, but it only takes a moderate gale to raise the wind chill factor to bring it to minus 30 degrees with a high risk of frostbite, and this assumes one hasn't got wet hands. Mostly we feared the boat icing up if we got caught while sailing in a gale. Frozen halyards would mean we couldn't

Above: Pauline makes the most of an idyllic day in Jason Harbour. Calm, fine weather is typical of winter, but it is interspersed with spells of savage winds and blizzards. Opposite: An isthmus at nearby Maiviken protects its waters from most of the glacial ice that streams out of Cumberland West Bay.

drop the sails, and further ice buildup would affect her stability. We might get driven out to sea, and the nearest feasible destination was South Africa, 3,000 miles away.

A photograph in Gerry Clark's book *The Totorore Voyage* is one of the most frightening and cautionary we have ever seen. He had been sailing around South Georgia in winter, counting penguins and albatrosses for the BAS, and making other valuable bird recordings. Leaving from the South Sandwich Islands, 300 miles farther southeast, he was caught in a severe gale at the end of September 1985. His 34-foot *Totorore* had been covered with ice to quite a few feet above the deck despite his and his crew's desperate efforts to chip it away. Steering be-

Antarctic winter's other side: when we are not battling the elements at sea,
we are exploring South Georgia's remote interior. Pauline ridge-walks near the summit
of an unnamed mountain above Glacier Col only three hours from Grytviken.

came impossible with the tiller and rudder frozen into a solid block and the boat began to get top heavy, wallowing and listing with an estimated 2 tons of ice on her. A chilling horror story with an awesome photograph to prove it. We had no ambitions for such a survival tale — life was much too good to take high risks and so we always tried to sail warily.

I N THE HALF-LIGHT *Curlew* AT LAST REACHED CAPE CONSTANCE after beating along the coast in strong winds and dodging ice from the Fortuna and Crean glaciers. We nervously watched the diameter of the rigging as it grew thicker with freshly forming ice where it reached the decks. They were getting slippery, too, as the seawater which washed over them quickly froze. Barely in time *Curlew* escaped into Blue Whale Harbour, hurtling along with the sails eased as though her life depended on it. We skimmed close along the edge of fringing rocks and there was just enough light left, reflecting from the snow, to pick out the anchorage and judge the distances off the shore.

"I'm not sure this winter cruising is such a good idea," I ventured, after *Curlew* was safely moored and I had stopped shivering with a combination of fear and cold. "No worries, mate," said Tim, sounding cocky as he put on his best pseudo-Australian accent now that the fire was warming up the icy cabin and his hands were thawing as they embraced a mug of tea, "we'll be as good as gold in here."

And he was right, though we lay to three anchors and the whirling dervishes spumed over *Curlew* yet again. It was the equinox, traditionally the time of the fiercest gales, and hundreds of miles to the north a Russian ship was sinking with the loss of all of her crew save one man. RAF Hercules aircraft were asked to search and rescue but to no avail. The BBC was reporting the drama while *Curlew* bobbed and weaved to the smoking winds that buffeted her on alternate sides. It seemed that the whole Southern Ocean had gone mad. Back in the most sheltered spot on the island the garrison recorded an unprecedented eighteen days of gale for the month of September.

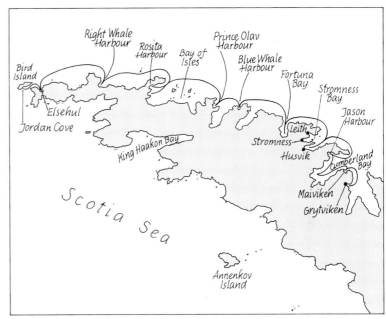

Cooped up and frustrated by the severe weather we debated whether to continue any further. Bird Island was still 40 miles away, sailing into the prevailing winds, and the breaks in the weather had been minimal. Even topping up with water was a feat in itself as it meant bailing snow into buckets and bowls and then slowly melting it over the stove.

"You have to take the rough with the smooth," Tim reasoned. "What smooth?" I muttered under my breath.

Prince Olav Harbour lay just across the notorious Possession Bay. "The windiest place in South Georgia," says the *Antarctic Pilot* cheerfully; however, we chose not to listen to it and turned down the earflaps of our sheepskin hats.

"Onward and upwind" ever we slogged, ducking into Prince Olav, Rosita, Right Whale Bay, and Elsehul to thaw out and catch our breath and enough courage for the next leg. "Do

Stranded glacial ice in Harpon Bay at the foot of Lyell glacier, one of three glaciers that meet the sea at the head of Cumberland West Bay.

you realize that we are probably the only idiots trying to sail in the Antarctic at this moment? Or for that matter *Curlew* is the only yacht anywhere south of the Polar Front?" It was a disturbing thought. "And somebody somewhere is sailing with warm sunshine on bare skin where the spray doesn't freeze and the next gale isn't imminent." Tim was even beginning to sound wistful, but at last all that lay between us and Bird Island was the sound. Its reputation is so awful that we were still doubtful of crossing the remaining and tantalizing 4 miles.

Above: Tim hammers in a piton on which to attach a mooring line from Curlew *onto George Rock. Despite this sheltered spot, we feel it necessary to lie to two anchors and a line ashore. It is difficult to take too many precautions when winter cruising.* **Opposite:** *Pauline raises* Curlew's *staysail as we set out on our first winter cruise along the northwest coast toward Bird Island.*

Chapter VIII

Albatross

October 1993

Keith, one of the men overwintering on the 3-mile-long Bird Island, was speaking into the handset of his radio to Stephen Palmer, dean of Christchurch Cathedral in the Falkland Islands. "No, we haven't seen Tim and Pauline, but the message was not to expect them for sure. The weather has been awful. I'm no sailor but I certainly wouldn't want to be out there. Today it's a bit warmer but I can only just see through the murk beyond the entrance to Jordan Cove . . . at least there's no ice around." He peered through the hut windows, past the expectant crowd of hungry skuas and a solitary preening penguin, in the

direction of the tiny pass, and, seeing white flashes of foam on the guardian reefs, his eyes narrowed suddenly, focusing on an unfamiliar shape, and then he laughed. "You won't believe this, Stephen, but *Curlew*'s sailing in now. Well, I'm" — he paused, remembering the cleric at the other end of the radio link — "blowed. Isn't that good news!"

It wasn't quite over for us yet as we strained to pick out the safe, deep water between the rocky edges of the pass. The fluky wind was likely to head us at any moment and there was little room to maneuver. *Curlew*'s wriggleability rose to the challenge as her heavy hull kept the momentum going between puffs and soon she was gliding into Main Cove, the dangers astern. Tim called for me to drop the jibs, and next the anchor, close to the entrance. Then I paid the anchor chain out freely beneath the boat as we sailed slowly along. At the same time Tim was dropping the mainsail and *Curlew* rounded up to lie facing the way we had come in. It felt very snug in the tiny bay, cut off from the sea by the reefs and a spit of land. We were overjoyed to be there.

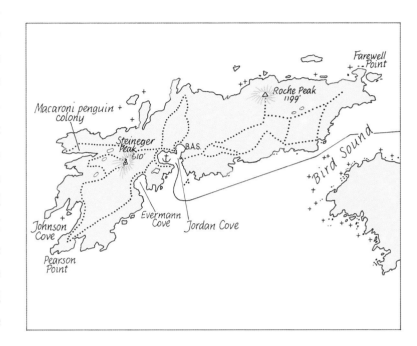

BIRD ISLAND

A couple of hours later when *Curlew* was trussed with mooring warps like the proverbial fly in a spider's web, we thought it safe to go ashore. Nick was at one of his albatross colonies high up on the hill that is charted as Stejneger Peak, but known to all BAS people affectionately as "Tonk." Nick came plowing down a drift-filled gully wearing snowshoes. In the hut Norman put the kettle on while Andy was working on the computers, setting up a new system that belied the little hut's primitive outward appearance. It was well heated, too, welcoming to the hard-working men after hours spent on exposed beaches or hillsides in bitter winds — days spent counting seals or birds, weighing them, checking tags and rings, and, in these sophisticated times, attaching and removing electronic monitors.

*Previous spread: A pair of gray-headed albatrosses (**left**) preen, and a wandering albatross sits on her nest (**right**). **Opposite:** Bird Island in all its splendor, with* Curlew *snug in a perfect harbor, a wandering albatross soaring nearby. Turbulent, tricky Bird Sound foams beyond the cove, with the mainland in the background, culminating in dazzlingly white Snow Peak (2,829 feet).*

Keith came to meet us, fresh from weighing a newborn elephant seal pup, and we watched to see the thin, shaggy-coated infant begin to suckle again from its placid, rotund mother. Keith's principal task would be monitoring the fur seal population but it was too early in the season for more than a few stragglers to be sitting around the beaches, so he was happy that this year a couple of elephants had pupped nearby.

He held out a muddy, sealy hand which we clasped warmly. It was great to see fellow humans after the month's hardships and the genuine welcome from the people on the isolated little base made all the struggle to get here fade.

*Above: This adult wanderer, just returned after a week or so at sea, feeds its excited chick. The chicks often tap the adult's bill to encourage it to regurgitate hot fish paste. **Opposite:** The older a wanderer gets the whiter it becomes, though its wing tips and edges remain black. Some 1,300 pairs of the great birds return to Bird Island every two years to breed.*

142

IN 1775 CAPTAIN COOK GAVE BIRD ISLAND ITS PROSAIC NAME "on account of the vast numbers that were upon it." On a summer day the green slopes are covered with large white dots looking like scattered sheep, but they are some of the 1,300 pairs of wandering albatrosses that return every two years, faithful to their lifelong mates, to breed and raise their young. Between breeding years Bird Island wanderers have been recorded in Australia. With their long life spans, comparable to a human's, they make several dozen circumnavigations in a lifetime. A humbling thought. Bird Island is also home to nearly 30,000 smaller albatrosses, vast numbers of penguins, petrels, and other seabirds, ducks, and the only songbird to be found in the Antarctic, the tiny South Georgia pipit.

The next week flew by in a blur of excitement and frenzy of whirring wings. Days were getting longer, the miracle of a new season's vibrant cycle beginning. Given the run of the island we hiked from narrow rocky cove to craggy vantage point, from luxuriating leopard seals sunning on the shore to the young wandering albatrosses overflowing their pedestal nests like giant poodles. Here, looking into their steady, serene eyes we could let the stress of the old month's violent weather roll off us — just like the snows that were fast melting away after the first thaws of a new month.

Above our heads the air was filled with the smaller albatrosses. Sometimes higher still we

would spot a great white cross against the lowering clouds, which signaled a parent wandering albatross returning from a long foray of many days to its chosen feeding grounds. This might be southern Brazil perhaps, if it was a female, more than 3,000 miles in just over a week, three times faster than *Curlew* could ever travel. If it was a male it would most likely be coming from Cape Horn and the furious fifties. Against the wind outward bound, making a mockery of our efforts in the same direction.

What a thrill to see the careful trial passes and dummy runs as the great bird with its 11-foot wingspan circled and tested the vortexes. Then it would abandon its mastery of the air to land rather less elegantly than a Concorde, generally in an undignified heap, nose down onto its 6-inch-long pink beak. I vowed then never again to criticize Tim for having several goes to pick up a mooring buoy or choose the exact spot to anchor in fluky winds. "What's good enough for the albatrosses. . . ."

The excited, whistling, eight-month-old chick would watch its parent during all these aerial maneuvers until the adult walked awkwardly from the landing strip — for that is what the mossy swards nearby really are — and settled down to pass beakfulls of hot fish paste into its wide-open gullet.

Norman took us to his gray-headed and black-browed albatross colonies and we watched them returning for the spring in ever-increasing numbers, sometimes landing virtually on our laps with no sign of fear or resentment. No sign of embarrassment either as they courted, preened each other's delicate feathers, billed ecstatically, and mated before our eyes. Both birds have impressive wingspans—almost 8 feet in the black-brow and just over 7 feet

The black-browed albatross returns annually to Bird Island to mate.
When the breeding season is over, South Georgian black-brows can be found
in the cold Benguela current off the southwest tip of South Africa.

for the gray-heads, who only breed every two years while the black-brows are annual breed-ers. This is probably because of their different diets and the energy they have to expend to reach their food. The gray-heads tend to fly toward the polar front looking principally for squid, whereas the black-brows forage along the shallower shelves around South Georgia and the South Orkney Islands, hunting chiefly for fish and krill. When the breeding season is over many of the South Georgian black-brows can be found in the cold Benguela current off the southwest tip of South Africa. South Georgian gray-heads have been recorded in New Zealand and Australia.

High above, lark-like, the little pipit which had been silent all winter trilled with appar-

Above: Mating gray-headed albatrosses. These birds sometimes landed virtually in our laps with no sign of fear or resentment, and mated before our eyes. **Opposite:** *A BAS scientist checks the birds' ring numbers, then records the data into a recorder.*

ent delight. Tinier than a sparrow, we wonder how this landbird survives the wind and cold. But it does so, and quite successfully, as long as there are no rats. The nest, tucked out of sight inside a tussock grass clump, is too vulnerable and the bird's size is too small to put up any fight against the brown rats that have invaded so much of the mainland. We never see pipits near the whaling stations, so their sweet song was a special treat for us.

The sun promised the warmth of spring, the petrels' breeding burrows began to thaw, and the green tussock grasses sprang through the winter snow cover. Looking down on *Curlew* from the ridges of Tonk our spirits soared too. Not only had the little cutter run the gauntlet of the winter's worst onslaughts and brought us to this avian heaven, but we spent some exquisite and intimate moments with the greatest of all the seabirds, whose oceans we share. To quote from American naturalist Robert Cushman Murphy, who sailed to South Georgia in 1912 aboard the sealing and whaling brig *Daisy*, "I now belong to that higher cult of mortals for I have seen the albatross."

The BAS blokes came to dinner on *Curlew*. They talked with sadness about the decreasing numbers of albatrosses. All the species as well as white-chinned petrels fall victim to the long-line fishing boats. Baited hooks on a 10-mile-long sinking line whirl off their drums and tempt the albatross into grabbing the baitfish, only to get hooked and dragged down into the depths to die. The wanderer population is decreasing at an alarming 1 to 2 percent a year despite efforts to persuade the fishermen to change their methods of fishing. Two leg bands handed in at Grytviken by fishermen who came in to take water last winter could be traced directly to two nests on Bird Island. The scientists could only watch sadly as the chicks starved with insufficient food, despite the efforts of the single parents, and died.

The outlook is grim. The South Georgia government specifies that lines of baited hooks should only be set at night and that the boats must trail streamer lines which scare off most birds. If these guidelines are followed only about three birds are caught per boat per month. But an official fisheries observer told us of another licensed long-liner fishing near Bird Island that was catching sixty birds per day — obviously not following the guidelines but apparently getting away with it. There are up to ten licensed long-line fishing boats catching the high-quality and valuable toothfish around South Georgia, with quite a few unlicensed poachers sneaking in among them. And then beyond the 200-mile limit there are more boats

This seemingly affectionate female wanderer approaches Pauline,
gently preens her, and then delicately removes her sunglasses.

with no restrictions imposed on them whatever. The majority of our wanderers are taken by fishing boats off southern Brazil and Uruguay, over which there is no control. Sometimes we feel quite desperate. The true cost of feeding the planet gets forever higher and harder to justify.

We spent a couple of evenings at the base. As though the day spent with albatrosses in the field were not enough, the men got out an old video of the first team to winter on Bird Island in 1963 and we watched a film on albatrosses. It told of how the earliest researchers had sprayed the birds' undersurfaces with bright pink dye so that they could be spotted by ships at sea — that is, if the seafarers were not too embarrassed to admit to seeing pink albatrosses!

All too soon it was time to leave. Duty called us back to Grytviken by mid-November, where we expected the arrival of the BAS research ship *James Clark Ross* on her first call of the season. The wind was fluky and Tim sailed *Curlew* in tight circles within Main Cove until he felt that a steadier breeze pattern was establishing. Keith, who had admitted to being no sailor, wondered if Tim was "winding *Curlew* up," building up momentum so that she could negotiate the tricky entrance at speed. If only it were that simple. But eventually she did pop out of the pass, like a cork out of a bottle, and then we were surging through Bird Sound again. Our nervous eyes flitted on the rearing breakers to starboard, the white, froth-fringed cliffs to port, and the woolen streamers on the rigging that told us how dangerously close we were to jibing the mainsail across the boat in a vicious uncontrolled slam. "Here we go," I thought. "Between the devil and the deep blue sea again!"

But *Curlew* easily covered the entire distance home in just the one day. A downhill sleigh ride in the sunshine, reaping the rewards of a fresh following breeze after the earlier month-long struggle upwind against all the elements.

WE RETURNED TO BIRD ISLAND A FEW MONTHS LATER, in high summer, to watch the wanderers displaying and dancing in groups of three or more with wide outstretched wings and clopping beaks, descending scale whistles, and curious *oinky-oinky-oinky* calls. I hung back as Tim photographed these graceful prima donnas and watched the overall scene with the Willis Islands forming a wild backdrop to the mossy stage. Occasionally a dancer would drop out and another one might take its place for a while until the first one rejoined the ballet.

One of the dropouts was heading my way. She (we learned later it was a she) placed her huge webbed feet carefully one in front of the other as though just learning to walk; her legs are not really designed to take such weight for long, wanderers being birds of the sky for months, often years at a time. It was a long walk and she never wavered in direction until she was gazing up at me fearlessly from less than an arm's length away. After some thought she picked up my 4-foot-long ski pole easily in her beak. Then she let it drop and nibbled at my fingers in their woolen mittens, working her way up the sleeve of my jacket until she got to the fleecy collar. This was more to her liking and she held on to it for a while. Then it was the turn of my hair and fleece headband and finally she preened my eyebrows as delicately as though her beak were just the size of a pipit's.

By this time Tim had turned the camera lens round onto this incredible sequence and was approaching slowly. I was holding my breath in excitement and certainly some nervousness at the proximity of that huge beak. The albatross reached for my gaudy pink sunglasses and ever so gently removed them from my nose. They were restrained by their cord so I slipped them back into place, to protect my eyes. Then she tried again, and again. Eventually, just as softly as she had approached, she wandered off and later we saw her rejoining the dancers.

A kiss from Pavlova could never have been so welcome. Or to paraphrase Robert Cushman Murphy: "I now belong to that higher cult of mortals for I have BEEN PREENED BY the albatross."

The courtship dance of the wandering albatross, with the Willis Islands in the background.
One of these three came over to preen Pauline just after this photograph was taken.
Note the nesting albatrosses on the steep, tussock-covered hillside beyond.

CHAPTER IX

ELEPHANTASTIC

September-December 1993

*T*HE FIRST SIGN OF SPRING is the return of the elephant seal bulls. They haul out onto the snow-covered beaches and claim territories in early to mid September, some of the females arriving by the third week. The bulls are in peak condition for they will have to live, fight, and mate during the breeding season without any new food supplies. So at this time it is possible for a superb specimen to weigh in at nearly 10,000 pounds — the females a mere 1,800. These are the largest seals in the world, and we would certainly argue the noisiest.

Just after we first arrived in Grytviken and tied *Curlew* up in the evening ready for a good night's sleep, a young bull decided to challenge her — or at least that is what it sounded like. Laying his chin against the planking he vented all his pent-up frustration into roaring as loud as he could. This effect pleased him as much as it displeased us. *Curlew* acted like an acousti-

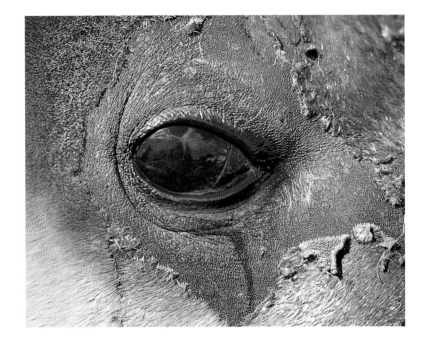

cal chamber for his efforts and so he tried again. In fact he tried most of the night so that we had little sleep and even less love for young bull elephant seals by morning.

The roar of an elephant seal is a deep, resonant, throaty gargle. . .magnified many-fold. Imagine trying to sleep with your ear a few inches away from a roaring animal that can still be heard several miles away. The young bull was so impressed with the sound of his own voice that he swam toward the lo-cal colony, a scant hundred yards from *Curlew*, to challenge the resident beachmaster. He roared again. But this time, without the echo-chamber effect, his roar impressed no one — especially not the alpha bull, who never even raised his head or rolled a bloodshot eye. Today's youth, really! So the young bull consoled himself with serenading *Curlew* — often.

Proximity to the colony had many advantages that outweighed a few disturbed nights — for we soon learned to sleep through most of it, as do people who live close to a main road. Generally in the mornings as we opened the hatch there would be a few hippo-like backs in the water, then conical heads, wreathed with folds of flesh and toothy grins, would slowly emerge and survey their surroundings. The mooring lines that stretched across the lit-tle basin where *Curlew* lies would catch a powerful body, like ropes in a boxing ring, until it stopped, backed off, and tried again.

Only once did a bull achieve any serious damage and that was when the dinghy lay along-

Previous spread: The first sign of austral spring is the return of the elephant seal bulls. The females — and mating, along with fierce fighting for primacy among the bulls — soon follow. Here a prime if battle-scarred bull mates as a pup looks on. **Opposite:** *Dueling bulls with a pup trying to get out of the way; many are crushed.* **Above:** *Molting skin of an adult female.*

side *Curlew* just as we were leaving to go for a sail. The fractious animal kept surfacing and roaring at us, to which we paid the usual scant attention. "Buzz off, bully boy." Then suddenly he pulled himself up as high out of the water as he could, gave us a wicked look of sheer defiance, and thrust his chest at the dinghy with all his weight behind it. There was an ominous flexing, cracking, and splintering of wood as the gunwhales split. Tim stood by with a boathook but, satisfied with his gesture, the bull slid under *Curlew* with a sideways swish of his hind flippers and swam away.

When elephant seal bulls fight they rear up almost onto their tails so that height is a major advantage. Then they can chop downward or sideways with their conical teeth carrying

An alpha bull, weighing in at almost five tons, amidst his harem. In the peak of condition, for the next two and a half months he will go entirely without food and mate with 80 or more females. **Opposite:** *A backward glance from a young bull.*

most of the weight of their massive bodies behind the blows. Most fights are short-lived skirmishes with the vanquished soon gauging his own inadequacy by the more powerful bull's greater height or even just by the pitch of his roar alone — and not necessarily volume. Hence there is always a fair bit of practicing for both roaring and sparring, which seldom ends in much bloodshed.

When a challenge is absolutely serious, with bulls well matched, it is quite awesome. A bull will arrive on the edge of a colony, quickly size up the beachmaster, and start to head his way. The alpha bull will plow off toward him in a straight line, which might be directly over panicking females, yelping pups, steep-banked streams, or any other obstacle — nothing, but nothing stands in the way of an elephant seal bull with tunnel vision. Then a dreadful, bloody battle will result, lasting for many minutes until one of the Titans, often minus an eye or large chunks of his nose and streaming blood across the snow, retreats back to the sea. Adult elephant seals very seldom die on the land, making strenuous efforts to return to the sea despite their injuries and sometimes vast amounts of blood pumping out of them. Tim witnessed one of these heavyweight title bouts and was amazed to see the victor turn immediately, after watching the vanquished one's retreat, to mate with the nearest female without pause for breath!

WHEN THERE HAS BEEN PLENTY OF SNOW in the previous winter and the colony has moved back from the immediate beach, the pups are often born onto snow several feet deep. It must be a shock to their systems, but they are designed for that. Thick black hair at birth helps to protect a skinny 80-pound body until the mother's rich milk — 40 percent fat content — begins to fill them out with a protective layer of blubber. By the time they are weaned, just after three weeks of age, they have become huge rounded butterballs and can weigh 400 pounds, while their mothers have slowly deflated to look almost slim and streamlined.

Before they achieve independence the pups can face death in an ironic form. Their body heat melts the snow and they begin to sink down into little holes from which they can never crawl out on their own. Eventually all that is left is a head bleating pathetically for food and a distressed, milk-bloated female watching helplessly over it. Often they drown in the meltwater beneath the snow. Sometimes a blizzard will cover them completely to be rolled over and squashed by their own mother who has, by then, completely lost touch with their whereabouts. But the logic of nature is that something else always gains — in this case the skuas, giant petrels, sheathbills, and gulls. Without this meat they couldn't survive or feed their own chicks and maintain their species.

There are over 300,000 elephant seals in South Georgia; there is little we can do except help in the immediate colony, and each year we have pulled out between ten and twenty pups from snowy graves. There is nothing so rewarding as watching the rescued pup start to suckle again, but sometimes it is quite traumatic reaching them.

"Are you going to do the pup patrol today?" I ask Tim. "Yes, it's early enough, I can do it on the way to work." He stops by the boat half an hour later. "Two are in, I can't get to one but it might get out on its own. We'd best give the other a go, it's a big one, we'll need the rope."

Wind, frozen snow, and low temperatures do not appear to affect these animals. The adults are well-insulated with their 4-inch layer of blubber and the pups are born with long black natal fur. Eighty pounds at birth, their mother's rich milk brings them up to 400 pounds within only three weeks, when they are ready to wean.

Thirty-eight females lie sprawled on the snow with the bull closest to the beach. "Silly old fellow, why don't you let them all go onto the beach where they'd be safe?" I wondered. "Probably because they're not his pups so he doesn't have a vested interest in their survival and by keeping the cows away from the water he's less likely to lose a few matings to peripheral bulls," Tim answered. Male logic.

We weigh how best to approach the pup-in-a-hole with minimal disruption to the other suckling females. Its mother eyes us warily as yet another reason to protect her pup, which she can barely see unless she puts her head right over the edge of the hole. There's water at the bottom and the pup is wet as well as stiff with the confinement of its icy tomb; hungry, too. Its eyes are closed but as the big human blocks out the light it rallies. I try to keep the mother occupied with the blunt end of my ski pole — I'd hate to harm her with the sharp end. She lunges at it while Tim drops a lasso of rope over her pup's wide-eyed black head. He jumps back, leaving the line slack, as the mother swivels around, no longer distracted. We play a waiting game and then approach from the other side. Tim jiggles the noose with long practice. "Gotcha." The rope slips under one flipper and he tightens it. I try to distract the female again as he stands over the hole and pulls up with all his strength.

Mwack, mwack, mwack the pup protests. *Huw, huw, huw,* the mother responds and then goes

for Tim with her equivalent of a roar, more of a loud gargle, really. But the deed is done, the pup has been dragged farther down the snow to more solid ground with the mother in full cry after it. All that remains is to loosen the noose and let the pup crawl out of it. We stand to one side like proud parents ourselves as the pup finds the teat and starts to make up for lost time. I turn moist eyes to Tim, both of us always slightly emotional on these occasions, but displaying it differently. "Thank you, love." "Quite okay. All in a day's work — speaking of which. . . ."

We wonder if we are interfering with nature yet again, since the snow may well be a natural way to cull the seals, who have so few enemies once they mature. But when it comes to compensating for the man-made hazards, there is little doubt.

The whaling stations present many traps to the more adventurous weaned pups (we call them weaners) as they investigate holes that have a fatal fascination and, of course, frequently fall into them. We found two in the floor spaces underneath a derelict building and one in an old barge — the manhole through which it had entered was scarcely big enough to fit it through on the way out with Tim pulling and me pushing. Another time we found one with its head through a hole in the whaler's bulwarks, stuck like a cork in a bottle with the tide rising over its head. We got thoroughly wet and coated with spilled furnace oil pulling that one back out, but there was not much time left for niceties. The whaler's tanks are supposedly empty but there is always a residual amount of treacly sludge that slowly leaks out from weeping rivet holes.

Opposite: Tim on pup patrol, rescuing a youngster from a snowy grave. The pups' body heat melts the snow from beneath them so that they "dig" their own graves. Each year we rescue 10 to 20 from this fate. **Above:** *A newly weaned pup.*

When Tim was off in the Falkland Islands, the soldiers came to me to say they'd found a seal in a large old whaling station boiler. They didn't think it could be got out since it had fallen in through the top and suggested that maybe the kindest thing would be to shoot it. They would be back in an hour. I investigated and found a frightened weaner about 5 feet down in its narrow-necked prison. I reassured myself that it hadn't yet learned how to use its budding teeth properly and went off for the rope.

When the soldiers returned I went down into the boiler with the seal. Despite its loud protests and attempts to defend itself, I fashioned a rope harness around its chest and neck, then passed up the other end. "Right, lads, pull!" said the major — and fourteen pullers, plus me in the tank as pusher, popped the 400-pound female out. She lay blinking in the sunlight while I untied her and the soldiers piled pallets and rocks over the entrance so it wouldn't happen again. The troops didn't know about weaners still having to learn how to grasp with their mouths. They just saw an angry red gape with teeth, and were very impressed with my "bravery." I didn't enlighten them in case they, too, tried putting their hands into seals' mouths.

A couple of weeks after the females have left their pups and gone to sea, the weaners all band together and begin to learn to swim. As they get more adventurous they progress around the cove shores, spending a few days in each area playing together and with anything that attracts their attention, such as fronds of kelp or feathers. The partially sunken whaler *Petrel* and *Curlew* offer all sorts of possibilities, too. We soon learned that the braver ones would play with our wriggling fingers as we reached down off the stern of the boat. Little whiskers would touch our hands as gummy mouths tried to "catch" them. But after a slightly more mature one did manage to draw a trace of blood we became wary.

*Opposite: Pauline among the milk-bloated weaners, left in groups, called creches, to fend for themselves when their mothers return to sea. **Above:** The bull pups are easily distinguished from the cows: Almost before they can move, they start fighting.*

You can quickly distinguish the bull pups from the cow pups. Almost before they can move, the young males start fighting. Of course it is totally ineffective and usually hilarious as they try to thump chests like miniature versions of their fathers but frequently miss completely and occasionally fall over backward. We even found one earnestly fighting a bright red door — maybe it saw its reflection. Eventually the combatants fall asleep, worn out like all toddlers, bodies contentedly close together.

WE HAD A VERY SPECIAL INTEREST IN ONE FEMALE PUP — let's call her Ellie. She was only a few days old, trying to swim and blowing bubbles, apparently in danger of drowning when we first saw her. Somehow she reached the tide line and stretched out, exhausted. A pup that age shouldn't be in the water, nor should she have been separated from her mother, but we had a lot to learn then and merely photographed her with interest. This first summer the colony was right down on the beach —

not because the bull had placed them there but because the soldiers were doing live-firing exercises.

A week later life was ebbing from her bony body; her coat was dusty, her eyes sunken with dull red membranes half covering them. After ten days she could barely raise her head to suckle pathetically from a protruding rivet on an old barge drawn up on the beach. The scavenging skuas jostled for a closer position and pecked at her head as she slept, leaving a circular wound on her forehead.

This was heartbreaking. Never practical, I ran back along the beach to *Curlew* and threw myself at Tim in a fit of tears. "Bottle-feed an elephant seal!" he exclaimed at my tentative suggestion. "It would never work. Better to let nature take its course." Tim is practical.

Regardless, I grabbed a spare, clean dishwashing bottle and a rubber band to soften the spout and made up a jug of extra-thick full cream milk from a tin. In no time I was back with Ellie. She was too weak to resist but showed little enthusiasm as I pumped half a gallon of the white liquid into her. The next morning when I carried the jug and bottle back she was still alive. I continued to feed her for several days. It seemed she was a little better — perhaps the milk had in some way counteracted the dehydration she must have been suffering. But there was no way I could give her another 300 pounds' worth of body fat and the long-term future looked bleak. "You can't keep this up," said Tim, eyeing our depleting supplies of milk powder. "I know," I admitted sadly.

Thankfully fate intervened. I didn't have the heart to go near the colony, dreading what I would see, but Tim came back from a visit delighted. Somehow Ellie had found enough energy to locate her mother. An old and apparently sick female with rheumy eyes and a snot-caked face was allowing Ellie to suckle blissfully. Eureka!

The milk powder must have kept Ellie alive just long enough and now she was beginning to thrive as I proudly watched over her progress. Ellie's mother was still laden with milk and

*When we first saw Ellie she was trying to swim in the shallows, distressed at having lost her mother. Eventually, greatly weakened and on the verge of dying, Pauline intervenes (**above**) and bottle feeds a thick powdered-milk mixture.*

running a couple of weeks late despite the little pup's enthusiastic attempts to drain her dry. By now all the other mature females had swum off into the food-rich depths of the Southern Ocean after mating with the old, one-eyed harem bull. Eventually he gave up on the wait for Ellie's mum to be ready for mating and he, too, disappeared to sea, compelled by hunger and

presumably sated by the other thirty-seven females he had mated with that month.

Within a couple more days the milk supply tapered off, her mother swam out to sea, and Ellie was alone.

Many of the adults head as far south as the Antarctic Peninsula to dive up to a mile deep for a period of close to two hours. Others head north, which we verified once when we found tropical goose barnacles firmly stuck to a newly returned female's skin. Back in their element, elephants are no longer messy, smelly, ungainly beasts but supremely efficient swimmers and divers. Only sperm whales can even begin to rival them for depths of dives and time spent below the surface.

With her mother gone, Ellie, now almost average weight, joined the other pups in play. She didn't mind me tickling her under her flippers and quickly accepted my self-appointed guardianship. One day she discovered *Curlew* and spent many days close by in the water or off the old slipway astern. She was readily identifiable from the scar on her forehead.

Eventually she moved farther along the shores of the cove and in front of the whaling museum where again she allowed us to stroke her as she sprawled in the midday heat. Finally in late December both Ellie and *Curlew* went to sea—the pup to forage on the coast for a time, while we headed to the south of the island.

Now four years later we look carefully at the faces of newly arrived females. I would so love to see that scar again and know that Ellie had survived the rigors of life in the ocean and made it to adulthood.

Above. *A bull elephant seal, freshly returned in early spring and ready to breed, roars to claim his territory.*
Opposite: Sparring young bulls begin their practice bouts long before sunrise.

CHAPTER X

The

MOUNTAINEERING

DIMENSION

Winter 1996

ONE WINTER TIM was able to experience some outstanding forays into the major peaks. This was thanks to the presence of Chris Marlow, sergeant of the Royal Marines and mountain leader by profession, remarkable climber by passion. When Chris arrived he took one look at South

Georgia, knew that he had come to a mountaineer's paradise, and set out for the summits at every chance. Sometimes he went alone but soon whittled down the keen and ever-available expeditioners to just Tim and Pat Lurcock.

We had always been tantalized by Mount Sugartop, 7,623 feet high and unclimbed from our side. It must be the loveliest mountain in South Georgia. In the summer of 1993 Tim had accompanied Crag Jones, a Mount Everest summiteer, to the top of the Lyell glacier, where they lived in a tent for five days of pretty awful weather. Nor could they find a route onto Sugartop itself because of frequent ice falls from the overhanging glaciers.

Tim was not overly impressed with the huge weights — everything they needed to survive for five days — that they had to lug up the mountainous terrain and back again. There was no reward but sleepless nights in a wildly vibrating tent as the high winds battered it. Crag had at least taken a book with him, foreseeing such a boring wait, but it was not much use to Tim since it was written in Welsh! "Never again," Tim vowed on their return as his backpack hit *Curlew*'s decks, still weighing 65 pounds despite all the rations he'd eaten.

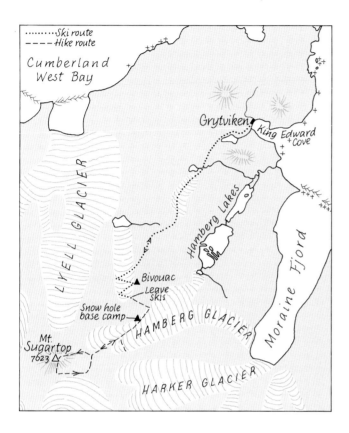

THE SUGARTOP
ROUTE

But a few years later here he was again with the map spread out, this time in front of Chris. Tim also showed him a sketch done by two young New Zealand climbers. They had found what looked to be a new route the previous summer but were prevented by time and weather from going any farther.

That was it. A few days later, in the cold, winter weather of mid-August, Chris, Pat, and Tim set off on their own recce. Leaving before dawn the three men were halfway up the eastern cirque of the Lyell glacier by the time Sarah, Pat's wife, and I skied to the top of Glacier Col to watch for them.

"Oh dear," Sarah said, lowering the binoculars wide-eyed, "I wish I hadn't seen that. I didn't think it would look quite so scary." Three tiny roped-up spiders were threading their way over recent avalanches and between icefalls and crevasses and heading straight up toward what looked like a vertical rock face. I must admit to taking an inward gulp, but promised Sarah that it wasn't as bad as it looked. Nevertheless, neither of us slept well that night.

In fact the men successfully climbed over the cirque onto a snow ramp leading to the Ham-

berg glacier, where they dug a luxurious snow hole for the night. Leaving again before dawn they crossed the Hamberg glacier. We believe it was the first time ever to have been traversed, although this is just an observation, not a milestone. Now they were truly on the mountain itself and well over halfway up. Some of the crippling weight from their heavy packs was left inside the snow hole so they could travel lighter and with more freedom to climb.

The summit lay less than a mile away but still a further 3,400 feet of difficult climbing. A very steep ice-filled gully, almost a thousand feet high, was ahead but gave access to a ridge that led to the summit. Chris, who is very experienced, was not fazed by the technical

Previous spread: The weather holds as Royal Marine Sergeant and veteran mountaineer Chris Marlow (left) and Pat Lurcock, Tim's climbing partners, climb to over 5,000 feet on a recce of 7,623-foot Mount Sugartop.

Above: Cocooned in our sleeping bags in a snug snow hole. Dug on the Hamberg glacier, it served us well as our base camp.

ice climb up the gully so it was very tempting for them all to push on. But time was not in their favor since a warship was due to arrive later that day, and they regretfully returned to sea level by dusk.

"That was probably one of the most exciting things I've ever done," Tim said, reliving it all at 3 A.M. the next morning as he lay in bed nursing aching muscles, drinking lots of rehydrating tea, and sharing more of the details. "It was extraordinarily beautiful up there, surrounded by huge crevasses and tortured ice masses being lit up by the rising sun. But one thing is for certain, there are no easy options and it is not surprising that it hasn't been climbed from this side before. Oh, and I forgot to tell you, there were snow petrels up there too, flying above the eastern cirque. It was late in the first day, the sun had sunk below the ridge, but it was still lighting the birds up. As they banked it shone a glorious flame color right through their wings — just magical."

Two weeks later they set off again. This is how Tim wrote about it for me so that I could better share his experience. I would have loved to be there but realize my limits for carrying heavy weights as well as having no serious mountaineering experience.

———————

CHRIS, PAT, AND MYSELF ARE BURDENED with weighty backpacks, heavier this time because this is the attempt and not the recce. We carry extra food, stove, fuel, safety helmet, clothing, but no tent. Each of us has a light, collapsible shovel for we plan to bivouac in a snow hole.

Side-slipping on the skis and traversing the first ice slope back down again after leaving Glacier Col at nearly 2,000 feet. Falling twice much to my chagrin. Difficult to get back up under the oppressive weight. Chris making it look easy with fluid, carefully judged turns.

More side-slipping and traversing down the well-named Killer Hill. Can't fall here, there is a several-hundred-foot drop with scree and rocks poking through icy snow. Inner leg tires quickly from digging the ski's metal edge into the icy snow to get some grip. I ask for a tad too many breaks on the ascent of Lyell's eastern cirque. Climbing again now, roped up, crossing a snow ramp so steep we have to do herringbone turns instead of

A day of rest and reconnoitering across the Hamberg glacier convince us that the risk from ice-falls along the east buttress of Mount Sugartop is too great for it to provide a viable route to the summit.

kick turns. Then we leave the skis and ski boots behind below the crest of the cirque, thinking it will be very nice to see them again in a few days. We all have rigid plastic mountaineering boots on now with crampons for grip into the firm névé snow. My ice ax hand getting very cold with frozen mitts while climbing the gully to go over the Col to Hamberg glacier; changed gloves.

Can't find the old snow hole left from the recce. Get really wet and tired after digging a new one and then blissfully climbing into a goose-down sleeping bag and quickly crashing after a vigorous day. Ten hours with little rest. Get up to a crackling clear day and a dazzling Sugartop. Roped up crossing the Hamberg glacier, now our second time, to a new lookout over the Harker glacier backed by the Henriksen buttress.

Amidst sparkling and wondrous surroundings we scan two gullies at the ridge leading to the summit of Sugartop. The eastern rock gully is topped by active ice cliffs, the northeastern looks feasible but scary. Reasonable rest the night before the beginning of the climb at 2 A.M. Setting off under the shadow of Surprise Peak — the shadow is cast by the light of a half moon. Bliss to walk with a lighter pack. A light freezing cold katabatic breeze wafting down the Hamberg, extremely cold to the exposed parts of the face, worrying a bit about Chris's feet, which are too cold. Change from headband to balaclava. It is minus 15 degrees without the wind, crusting ice under the nostrils. Making good time across the Hamberg with Chris still trying to get his feet warm. It is exciting and enchanting to cross a glacier at night with a rising half moon. Just the scrunch of footsteps in the dry snow and the squeaky whine of the lower tips of the ice axes as we plant them. Looking up at Sugartop's dramatic peak in the moonlight, it occurs to me that, for my first serious attempt at mountaineering, this is not really the right one to start with.

Above: We discovered this crystal cave when Chris fell into a crevasse. Opposite: It served as Pat and Tim's shelter as they waited for Chris to make his solo attempt of Sugartop's summit. The ice climbing had proved too challenging for the two novice mountaineers.

Less breeze as we start to ascend the other side of the Hamberg glacier toward the steeper gully. Chris's feet are still a problem. We reach the last crevasse and it is a major one. Chris shows me a body belay since I am the middle man. Pat tries to cross a thin snow bridge and his foot goes through. We move farther along to what looks like a better bridge. Chris tries to cross belly crawling and with arms and legs spread, trying to distribute his weight throughout, and then, with a shout, goes through and out of sight. I hang on with the body belay. Pat calls, "Are you okay?" Silence. Then Chris replies, "Come on in — it's great in here!" and he is standing on a firm snow slope inside the crevasse surrounded by frosty stalactites that are lit by the moon through the hole he has just made. Crystal magic.

Chris gets his boots off and warms his feet in Pat's armpits and I give him a spare pair of thick socks. We have a brew — hot soup from a flask. Then carry on with Pat leading so Chris can at least have his feet less constantly in the snow following our footprints, especially mine, size 12. He can stamp a lot because we are traveling slower now, going up the ever-steepening gully and being less fit than Chris. At one point Pat says, "Stop and look behind," and the moon has cast a beam through the morning fog onto the glacier — a surreal column of light and quite mystical. As we go on I am aware that we are higher than Surprise Peak and realize this is a milestone in itself. I never would have thought to be so high, over 5,000 feet, unless by helicopter, and that would be an insult to this precious place.

Chris's feet are numb and I am beginning to think we should abort. It is sickeningly steep and a long way down. Ice cliffs and seracs tower over us like sentinels. I reach my limit; too spooked to go on. We are about to change from snow to ice and I can't handle it. I am slightly comforted by Pat saying he is feeling somewhat the same and needs Chris to take over and lead over the ice. Chris is very disappointed but understands. We start to descend.

But then soon after Chris says, "Wait a minute, I'll go solo if that's okay with you." It

*Opposite: Tim at the highest point reached on the recce so that Chris could check the gully for the attempt at the summit of Sugartop. **Above:** Tim jumps a crevasse during the pre-dawn descent.*

is, and he casts off the rope for us to carry on down. It seems very final. Without any rope now and with an ice ax in each hand he goes "tack, tack, tack" up a steepening face into what is left of the night. Then there is a glow of another spectacular dawn.

Pat and I tread gingerly back to the crevasse cave and wait for Chris. We sit outside and warm our booted feet and gloved hands with the rising sun, overlooking the most incredible mountain and glacierscape view. Pat notices the moisture of the air freezing, floating and sparkling in the sun's rays. I see, by a trick of the light, a purple ice window — a hole through the crevasse appears to be colored by new light entering the cave.

It is so silent that you hear the blood pumping around your ears. The fog has all but cleared; some drifting, fair-weather cumulus clouds below us and over the sea are the only thing that moves — otherwise the whole earth has stopped moving. There is not a sign of human existence anywhere except our track disappearing toward the snow hole, across the glacier. We both sleep a bit but small nuggets of ice intermittently bombard us; then the occasional larger, brick-size one goes whizzing by. Not eager to give up our place in the sun's warmth we take our chances until I see a large piece spinning down, as big as a train wheel. This prompts us to take to the lower part of the slope where it becomes more gradual and shows less ice debris.

After several hours Chris appears like a flea on a polar bear, weaving in and out of the ice cliffs and seracs—a totally different route to the one we went up. The sun has really heated up and we both watch with some apprehension as he comes down all sorts of avalanche-prone funnels. It is a relief when he connects with our track in the main gully. We go up to meet him. As we do so a sizable avalanche smokes its way down not more than a couple of hundred yards from us—mostly ice pushing a vanguard of snow.

Chris jumps the crevasse with ease. He is having a big high. Deeply felt congratulations from us. What a bloke, nerves of Kevlar and climbs like a gecko. He says it is the most beautiful mountain he has ever seen, ice-domed summit with fluted ice that had to be knocked off with his axes and crampons as he did the final push. Sugartop had the good weather but most of the island was cloud-shrouded with just the higher peaks poking through. He tells us that the Christopherson glacier on the other side of the range looks to give much easier access.

We set out for our first attempt on Mount Roots (7,483 feet), the last major peak in South Georgia to remain unclimbed. It was described as "precipitous in the extreme" by Duncan Carse, leader of the 1951-57 survey team.

I make Chris tea and he falls into a deep, untroubled sleep, the indented stress lines on his forehead erased. This man earns all my respect — to me he is a gladiator.

At dawn next morning the last candle snuffs just as we are ready to leave. The snow hole has sagged on one side of the roof so that there is only enough room for feet under here. A dawn rappel over the Col onto the eastern cirque. A solitary, silent snow petrel swings close by then turns up into the new sun's light. I catch Chris's face looking up at it and for a brief instant I find it sad that this mountain hero has also been trained to go to war with fellow human beings.

Hello, skis — covered in hoar frost. We rope up for the last time and backpack the

Mount Paget just pokes out of the mist above the two-mile-wide snout of Nordenskjöld glacier, the widest in South Georgia.
Our route to Mount Roots leads us directly up Nordenskjöld on skis, with Pat hauling the pulk.

skis down the steep snow ramp to more manageable slopes, then a nice ski slide down the rest of the cirque to Killer Hill. I try crampons, the others go for skins on their skis. For once I made a reasonable choice. Chris and Pat take a worse pasting than I — they could do without that — there's still a bit of a slog left.

A lone figure in the distance. It is Pauline bringing fruit, cheese, homemade bread, and cheery chatter that warms us all. She loads up with some of my weight. The ski down the Col was brilliant, the air full of large fluffy snowflakes. We spot Sarah coming up the moraines. There is a good spirit in our small party. We are knackered but happy. On to *Curlew* for that barrel of beer and Sarah has even brought champagne.

Deep sleep till midnight then talk and tea. Pauline wants to know every detail. I want to tell it. She sympathizes with my short-lived disappointment at not reaching the summit but I am recovered now and savor the other countless rewards. Make love and doze until dawn. As I ski to work with aching calves, I pause and look up to Sugartop but it is not there; completely covered by cloud. The stunning view, looking through the derelict whaling station at the mountain, has lifted our spirits so many times. And now it has robed itself again. None of us will mock it with flags or tales of conquering prowess. Only Chris was allowed to reach the daunting summit, but such a privilege just to be allowed to reach its shoulders. I shall always regard Mount Sugartop with utmost reverence.

TIM HAS PERSISTED WITH THE MOUNTAINEERING, saying "Never again" less frequently. With the addition of Andy, one of the young signalers, the three would-be summiteers and Chris skied up the entire 7-mile length of the Nordenskjöld glacier, an awesome expanse of crevassed ice and virgin ski territory. There they set up their base camp, two tents dug well into a square pit cut out of the snow and surrounded by a wall made of blocks of snow from the diggings. Next day, despite strong winds, they headed toward the unclimbed Mount Roots, 7,483 feet and described as "precipitous in the extreme" by Duncan Carse, the leader of the 1951–57 surveying teams .

The early plan had been to make a reconnaissance trip on the second day so the men were not carrying much in the way of food and liquid. When Chris decided that they should go for the climb right then, Pat felt it would be more prudent to stop and stayed with young Andy to dig a snow hole at the base of a very sheer buttress.

In retrospect, he made the right decision because Chris and Tim climbed for a further twenty hours with only one brief halt. They were ascending a face sheltered from

the wind but overhead the clouds were spinning past at dizzying speed and Tim believed that the summit would have been untenable. Even down in King Edward Cove Sarah and I were very worried as spindrift spumed across the water and the garrison recorded 60 knots. Chris was hoping that the wind would moderate but it was not to be.

During the night the full moon had a total eclipse, casting an ominous darkness over the stark scene. At 2 A.M., and at a height of over 6,000 feet, Tim reached his limit again, not surprisingly, for this was his first pause in twelve hours, the only place where he could slip off his backpack and reach for the last of his food, drink, and much needed extra layer of clothing. But scarcely a relaxing break while balancing precariously bestride an icy ridge, with the snow dropping away on either side to oblivion. To make things worse the cloud now came down and covered their route.

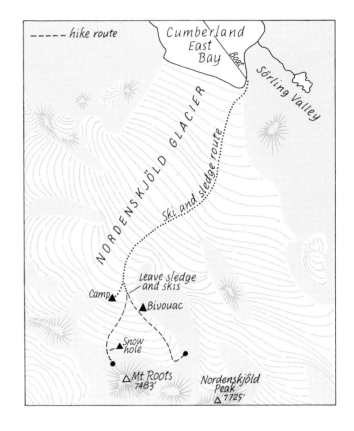

This time the climb had been much more difficult and technical than what Tim had experienced on Sugartop but in the meantime he had been practicing at lower levels. Like Chris he was using an ice ax in each hand and digging in the front points of his crampons at every step while his calf muscles screamed silently. They did about twelve pitches on the way up — a pitch is the length of a standard climbing rope, 165 feet — belaying each other continuously with pitons, ice screws, strops, and the cryptically named deadmen. Chris led on the way up, Tim on the return.

THE MOUNT
ROOTS ROUTE

After the first pitch Tim had called up to Chris, "What's the next bit like?" Chris's pause spoke volumes but eventually the reply came. "Easy." When Tim reached Chris's spot, his heart sank. If this was "easy," what was "difficult" going to look like? So after that he didn't ask anymore.

Toward the end they had to be so careful, both very tired and aware that their judgment could be impaired. In fact, Tim found himself nodding off for brief moments as they slowly descended and realized that he had no reserves left. Their climb was meant to end as

Our bivouac site on the eastern ridge of Mount Roots. We have just returned from our third attempt on the summit. This climb proved to be much more difficult and technical than the Sugartop expedition.

a planned glissade — a controlled slide down a snow slope. But it turned into a series of cartwheels as Tim, still roped up to Chris, plummeted down the incline, which was much steeper than they had thought. He was dragging Chris behind him, neither able to get an ice ax to hold and both worried about their flailing feet putting a crampon tattoo into the other

man. Then they collapsed into laughter at the bottom as much from the easing of tension as anything else.

Pat and Andy were very relieved to see them coming down as the wind was now reaching even to the snow hole. So, after a hurried snack and drink, they continued back to base camp — now twenty-nine hours since they had set off and Tim almost hallucinating with exhaustion and lack of sleep. Both tents had been blown down, but mercifully not away. With Pat and Andy working fast it was not long before everyone was fed and Tim and Chris were asleep, oblivious to the screaming gale outside and the barrage of granular snow slamming against the tents.

The next morning, ironically, dawned calm and beautiful. But there was neither food nor energy for any further climbing. Instead the four of them skied the whole length of the Nordenskjöld glacier again, skimming back down with a frozen snow crust supporting them over the crevasses. Pat had the pulk in tow the whole way since he was now the freshest after his enforced period in the snow hole and Andy's skiing experience was limited. As they telemarked down to the beach the army boats were landing to pick them up. "Did you crack Mount Roots?" asked one of the soldiers. "No," said Tim, "I think Mount Roots cracked us!"

Opposite: Looking down the Nordenskjöld glacier to Cumberland Bay from the bivouac site.
Above: A great release of tension as we celebrate Chris's successful climb of Sugartop.
From left: Pat, Chris, Tim, and Pat's wife, Sarah, share Champagne.

CHAPTER XI

JUST TALKING

to the

BIRDS

W

E ARE WALKING TO WORK EARLY on a

summer morning and high up in the sky a dark bird circles like

a lazy hawk. As we leave the narrow walkways between the old

buildings and reach the wide-open space in front of the mu-

seum the bird closes its wings and spirals down to whir past our

heads and land heavily at our feet. "Good morning, Skua!" He

("it," really, since skua sexes are indistinguishable to all but

skuas, but we decide "it" is a "he") flies alongside us, a few yards away at shoulder height, and then slews sideways like a kite on a string. After a while he prefers to scuttle on the ground, more like a large brown rat. We leave him at the back door of the museum where he waits hopefully for scraps — one beady eye on the rat runs in case an unwary one makes a dangerous daylight excursion. And he has proved a very efficient waste disposal unit on the occasions that we have caught a rat and passed it on to him. He gulps down the smaller ones whole but takes the larger ones to a furtive hiding place where he can digest in peace and without any competition.

Previous spread: *The little snowy sheathbill has an uncanny ability to intrude on Tim's photographs, this one grabbing attention from a pair of blue-eyed shags.* **Inset**: *A northern giant petrel chick.* **Above**: *Skua among the burnet flower heads. This skua became our friend, hanging about Curlew (**right**), especially when something smells good in the galley.*

Any skua-like rival is discouraged by his Viking pose. He lifts his wings almost vertical to display the large white flashes across them and screams a strident *chack-chack-chack*.

There is a lucrative krill fishery around South Georgia in the winter as the pack ice moves north and the krill with it. It is probably unfortunate that the Japanese have discovered how to remove the toxic amounts of fluoride that are harmful to humans and are now processing delicious frozen slabs of solid krill meat — just like shrimp meat. The Russian factory ships are canning it, too, so we hope that it doesn't herald yet another boom-and-bust fishery heading for overexploitation with catastrophic consequences to all the whales, birds, and seals that depend on it.

The processors are proud of their delicious new product and we have been offered generous samples from the fishing trawlers. One way or another, by skill, cunning, and sheer winsomeness, Skua has had more than his share of this bonanza. So much so that he would sometimes walk around with an empty tin of "Antarctic shrimp" in his bill, dropping heavy hints to us and illustrating a bizarre loop in the food chain.

Sometimes Skua follows us for the five-minute walk between the museum and *Curlew* and seldom bothers to fly much of the distance, running along at a slow walking pace like a terrier at our heels.

One day I was dusting the altar at the far end of the church and turned around to see Skua standing on the altar steps. His head was cocked to one side as he looked up, perfectly confident — all God's creatures!

Skuas are powerful animals, about 25 inches long, similar to gulls, but with a distinct hint of a bird of prey. They have been described as webfooted hawks. Their distribution is worldwide but in the Northern Hemisphere they are fairly difficult to see and a bit of a treat for birders. Skua cashes in on this and poses for the tourists, receiving lots of admiration and hoping for handouts. Unfortunately they are not so likely to have rats, pieces of reindeer meat, or fish guts in their packs so after a while he gives up and returns to his vigil at the museum back door. Maybe Skua is an immature since he never behaves as though he has a home. No mate to relieve or nest and chicks to care for.

The last time we saw Skua was after the first snows when we were skiing on the local hillsides. He spotted us from high above and came spiraling down like a damaged helicopter to crash-land in an inelegant flurry of snow. It was not a good place to stop so we carried on for a while with Skua battling along up to his chest in the fresh snow. Even the offer of sharing our pâté sandwiches with him did little to mollify his patent disgust at the wintry conditions, and shortly after that he must have headed north.

Skuas migrate toward the South American coast but a few birds have been seen as far north as California, Greenland, and Japan. They revert to their pelagic lives once the majority of South Georgia's wildlife has also gone back to sea and the food opportunities ashore have ceased. They are the first birds to return in September and the last to leave around April. A skua has been recorded almost at the South Pole — although a slightly different species than the South Georgian ones, which are known as brown or Antarctic skuas as opposed to the more southern South Polar skuas.

When we go walking in the summer, the blunted ski poles that we carry to discourage fur seals from biting are also useful hoisted a little above our heads to confuse skuas. They swoop in like small fighter aircraft, usually out of the dazzling sun and frequently from behind. They are normally very powerful and precise fliers with many scalps to their credit where humans have strayed too close to their nests, which they defend bravely. One or two chicks is the norm and the timing of hatching is usually related to the food supply. If they intend to live off the afterbirths and casualties among the elephant seals they will breed much earlier than if their nearest food supply is from a later-starting macaroni penguin colony. It is fascinating to watch a pair of birds cooperating in a sort of tug-of-war to pull and tear apart pieces of meat, which is so much more efficient than if they had worked individually.

*Opposite: Eastern European trawlers trans-ship hundreds of tons of krill (**above**), engine of the Antarctic food chain and, recently, favored food in Japan, creating a lucrative market and the threat of over-fishing.*

The least endearing skua trait is to live off the smaller petrels that return to their burrows at dusk. The first alert that you are in the breeding site of these birds is a random scattering of dozens of individual wings, all that is left of the victims and identifiable by their colors, dove gray for the dove prions, bluer and slightly larger for the blue petrels, and al-

most black for the diving petrels. Once we sadly found two perfectly white snow petrel's wings. All grist to the skuas' voracious mill.

We use the same anti-fur-seal, anti-skua poles to keep terns at bay, too, although we try to avoid any area where the birdlife is obviously being alarmed by our presence. Terns will all lift off together and fly a considerable distance to chase away any marauder, which includes humans, so that it can be hard to know which route is the least disruptive. While this is going on the eggs or youngsters are very vulnerable to any of the scavengers. Antarctic terns breed on small hilltops within plains and valleys and do not have a nest as such, just a scrape in the ground. Their mottled gray eggs are well camouflaged and could easily be stepped on by the unwary trespasser. They stay around the island in winter strengthening pair bonds and displaying to each other. Their migratory cousins, the Arctic terns, occasionally visit South Georgian waters in our summer clothed in their winter, non-breeding plumage but feeding well offshore since they have no need to come to the land to breed.

L IKE THE SKUAS, GIANT PETRELS ARE ALSO SCAVENGERS. But unlike the brown bombers they are normally fairly nervous birds, despite their size—nearly 3 feet long with a 7-foot wingspan. On land they are very ungainly and cannot take off easily without taking a long run at it and waddle away unhappily if you come across them

*Opposite: A nesting southern giant petrel and two bystanders. Vulture-like in their scavenging ways, they are related to albatrosses. **Above**: An Antarctic tern feeds its chick. These terns stay around the island in winter strengthening pair bonds. Their migratory cousin, the Arctic tern, occasionally visits South Georgian waters in our summer.*

sitting on the beach or hillside. There are two kinds in the world and both are here, only easily distinguished close up by the tips of their bills. Northern giant petrels have reddish coloration, whereas in the southern species it is green. The northerners breed about six weeks earlier, perhaps because they are adapted to a warmer, generally subantarctic climate and are at the extreme south limit of their range.

The soldiers at King Edward Point generally jump to the conclusion that giant petrels are albatrosses and go away with a very poor impression. If you approach the nest of a giant petrel too closely, as soldiers invariably will, the adult bird ejects a jet of foul-smelling oily liquid as a defense mechanism. They will tell you that it is very effective! The brindled plumage is less attractive than that of the other "tubenoses" — albatrosses and petrels — but very rarely you can come across one in what they call a white morph, found only in southern giant petrels. This is quite lovely, either pure white or with a random smattering of black diamonds. Just by that change in coloration, from an uninspiring gray-brown to a distinguished ermine, people's attitudes to the bird also change.

Nevertheless, whatever their color, "GPs" provide a macabre spectacle as they close in on a floating carcass. With great hunched shoulders trailing arched wings and tails turned back and fanned out like a turkey, they growl and screech to defend their bloody dinners. Reaching inside the dead animal for the tastiest morsels, their heads and necks are soon bright red with blood until only their pale eyes glare back unstained. They look like devil's apprentices, Tim suggested once, or animated gargoyles. Certainly they are the vultures of the Southern Ocean.

Another bird that scavenges, and has been looked down upon since the earliest sealers first described it, is the snowy sheathbill. It is their habit of sometimes recycling the resources, eating excreta, that mostly offended the squeamish whalers and sealers. How ironic

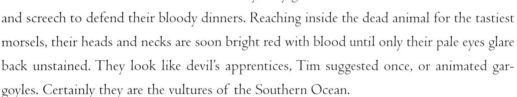

Opposite: An unusual white morph giant petrel with chick. Note the powerful "tubenose" bill, a characteristic petrels share with the albatrosses. Above: The sheathbill is a pigeon-like scavenger. In summer it feeds in the penguin colonies trying to get eggs. In winter it resorts to marine organisms, though in hard times it will migrate to South America.

to think of mass butcherers and exterminators condemning this efficient little cleanup merchant for its ordained niche in life. These pigeon-like birds don't have webbed feet, like seabirds, yet some of them make long ocean crossings migrating to South America when the food sources dry up. Others stay around South Georgia throughout the winter principally feeding off marine organisms and algae on the shoreline. In summer they feed in the penguin colonies trying to get eggs, but also will steal any food dropped between penguin and chick.

They have a knack of getting their picture taken and often when we are checking our returned photographs we find an impudent mutt staring into the camera lens, quite stealing the thunder from some rarer or more photogenic species. They are bold and curious and frequently investigate boots, skis, or anything else unnatural lying around. *Curlew's* compass is protected by a large white plastic dome which frequently brings mutts on board to hammer away at it with their tough little bills in the hope of cracking what they see as a giant egg. Sheathbills nest in burrows, clefts, or caves and once we saw them disappearing into a cavity under the jetty at Grytviken. They can rear several chicks.

There are two types of ducks here — as far south as ducks have been recorded. The South Georgia pintail is everywhere close to sea level in small groups, occasionally gathering in flocks of up to a hundred. The whalers used to shoot and eat them but there wouldn't be a lot of meat on these delicate little beauties. They don't quack but make a subtle little *brrreep*, like a subdued telephone. They have been reported and even photographed eating meat from dead seals — the only carnivorous duck in the world as well as the southernmost.

After a year here we noticed another type of duck, so similar in appearance that we might be forgiven for not spotting the difference. Speckled teal were first observed at King

The South Georgia pintail is the southernmost duck in the world, and stays on the island year-round. It is everywhere close to sea level in small groups, and occasionally gathers in flocks of up to a hundred. It doesn't quack but makes a subtle little brrreep, *like a subdued telephone.*

Edward Point in the early 1970s when there were about a dozen birds. It is assumed that they blew downwind here by accident from the Falklands or South America, but they have adapted to the more severe climate and survived if not exactly thrived. We have only seen thirteen birds, thought to be the entire population, which come by *Curlew* in the winter to

brighten the coldest days by probing the floating ice lines, usually frozen by then, for seaweed or sea creatures. They all plump down to snooze on the ice like a series of little wooden decoys, carefully slipping their feet up and under their wings to keep them warm while just their downy bellies are in contact with the cold surface. They are much more nervous than their slightly larger cousins the pintails. Perhaps this is because they originated more recently from the Falklands and South America, where they are still targeted by hunters. Their call is different too, more of a piping whistle, and the first time we heard all thirteen birds vocalizing together it sounded like a long-forgotten dawn chorus and brought us rushing on deck to look for vagrant songbirds.

The other overwinterer is the blue-eyed shag, a widespread bird whose curiosity and fearlessness were nearly its undoing. The sealers and whalers favored it in their stewpots and could approach close enough to knock it off rocks with stones or even sticks, before the days of guns. When we are out at sea they will often detour miles to fly around and around and around *Curlew* and on a couple of occasions have hit the rigging because they weren't quite looking where they were going. In spring they fly doggedly to and from their colonies with enormous beakfuls of nesting material obscuring their view and then present them to their mates, displaying ecstatically and weaving long necks together like snakes enchanted by a snake-charmer. At first sight these black-and-white birds seem quite ordinary until you get close enough to see the vivid blue eye ring. Golden caruncles at the base of their bills,

"This is your early-morning wake-up call!" Gullible, our near-pet kelp gull, proclaims his territory from Curlew's *boom end at first light.*

combined with a crest in the breeding season and a hint of iridescence to their dark plumage, further enhance them.

None of these species has the charisma of an albatross or the drollness of a penguin but every creature on the island has an important role to play; they add variety and interest and, apart from the departed skuas, brighten our winters.

D URING THE EARLY PART OF OUR FIRST WINTER we found ourselves drawn to a kelp gull raising its fledgling chick. There was only one parent so we came to terms with "interfering" with nature, preferring to call it "helping."

The parent bird would stand on the boom end with one leg shaking and shivering pathetically, looking sideways at the solid ice which prevented it from feeding both itself and its youngster on their staple diet of limpets. It may well be that in a completely natural circumstance there wouldn't be kelp gulls here in the winter because this cove tends to freeze up as it is so sheltered. Then they would move to more turbulent areas where food is always accessible. But all gulls are highly opportunistic and scavenge wherever possible, and Grytviken has long been a source of easy pickings.

"Listen to this," I told Tim, reading from the fascinating book *Antarctic Isle* by Niall Rankin, long out of print. "When he visited South Georgia for the summer of 1946–47 he was able to photograph and take notes on all the breeding wildlife species without a hide — with the exception of the kelp gulls who were exceedingly nervous." "How I wish," Tim said.

Our two kelp gulls, Parkinson and Gullible, made an efficient alarm clock, arriving at first light with two heavy thumps on the boom end to loudly proclaim their rights over the area. "Elephant seals roaring all night, weaners thumping the fenders, and then these infernal birds cockadoodledooing in the wee small hours just after I've finally got to sleep! It will be great when winter comes and we won't be such nervous wrecks!" said Tim. "Bliss!"

On good days they foraged happily and naturally on the nearby shore and among the kelp, regularly swallowing whole limpets an inch or more in diameter. Then they regurgitated the shells later after digesting the meat. *Curlew's* decks were often the beneficiary of these. What stomachs they must have! What tolerance we needed.

During the first winter Gullible begged continually from his parent, making pathetic mewing noises as the adult struggled to feed a chick that seemed larger than itself. The mewing tended to get monotonous and a bit annoying and I used to condemn it loudly, shouting "Pathetic."

One day my booming "Pathetic!" happened to coincide with the new major's early attempts at skiing. He was in the process of picking himself up from a slow-motion teetering

fall down a snowdrift onto the slipway astern of us. I caught his expression as he looked across at *Curlew* following my sweeping condemnation. Uh-oh! It was a week before I could explain to him that I wasn't talking about him, nor was I having a row with Tim, just talking to the birds. . . .

When Tim fished for Antarctic cod through a hole in the ice, Gullible was there to assist. But first he had to learn how to handle himself on ice, with hilarious results. He would dig in his claws, on the end of his webbed feet, and glide off sideways in the opposite direction to which he wanted to go, wings flailing wildly, beak plowing a furrow.

One day Gullible saw a leopard seal hunting in the water around *Curlew*. His reaction was

Opposite: Gullible makes an ungainly landing as he learns to cope with ice during his first winter.

Above: The second winter with us, and Gullible's plumage has lightened. Is he becoming too trusting for his own good?

immediate, staring intently at the powerful animal and exhibiting all the signs of alarm and fear and drawing his body up into a tightly stretched, tall, thin shape. How is it, we wondered, that the menace of this seal could be communicated so strongly to a free-flying bird far beyond the seal's grasp. But Gullible immediately knew the presence of danger even

though this was probably the first "lep" he had ever seen. Our daily Weddell seal visitor and the elephants and fur seals never provoked such a reaction from him.

By the first spring he had learned to make a passable adult call, although his voice would break and give him away. His feathers had lightened so that he looked unmistakably like a gull although not the perfect dazzling white and contrasting black of the adults. His bill was a buff version of his parent's but without any yellow or hint of the bright red spot that the adults have. Nor did he have the red eye rim that denotes the breeding birds. But he was bold and strong

and chased the newly arrived skuas away with confidence. Parkinson considered a brief flirtation with Butterfly, a scrawny, lean, hungry bird, who nevertheless could delicately lift a knob of butter from my fingers on the wing. That's when we learned that Parkinson was a he. But nothing came of it the first two years — maybe Parkinson was still mourning a lost mate.

One night we had been to visit Pat and Sarah. As we were walking home there was a scuttling and fluttering on the ground. In the light of our headlights we could see a fledgling Wilson's storm petrel, still with a little of the chick down amid the feathers. Certainly rats would get it if we left it there so Tim slipped the tiny thing into his pocket. Perhaps it was not much different from the burrow it must have left a day before, and it chirped and begged all the way home. After about sixty days spent in a rock crevice or burrow high on a scree mountainside safely away from rats, the chick is abandoned by its parents. Eventually hunger forces it out of the nest to teach itself to fly and cope with the harsh world. If it survives to reach the sea and then learns how to feed, it must face one of the most distant migrations known, reaching as far as the coasts of New England in the United States. This tiny, delicate, mothlike bird dances on the turbulent oceans pattering its tiny feet across the

swells to the admiration of all of us who are buffeted by and know the power of relentless storms.

Back on the boat we examined the minute little scrap with awe. It had bright orange webs to its feet. Tim found that it was covered with burrs from the burnet plant which had clogged its wings and tail and effectively grounded the poor thing. He gently teased out the burrs, put it in a small cardboard box for the night, and gave it some butter and water. In the morning it began to preen itself and looked a little brighter — although still very young to have left home. "Best we let it go," said Tim (you know, the let-nature-take-its-course man), and opened the forehatch. It fluttered unsteadily away. We watched it proudly and smiled with smug satisfaction. Another good deed done.

White flashes on powerful wings, Skua makes a fine figurehead for Curlew.

Zap! Gullible had swooped and killed it as easily as if it were a pat of butter. Nature take its course, indeed. And to add insult to injury, exactly five days after a dark mass of feathers was regurgitated into the middle of the hatchway — with two little orange webbed feet sticking out of it!

When we went away sailing the first year Gullible and Parkinson would land on *Curlew* as soon as we returned, even before the anchor was dropped. The next year Gullible would come flying along behind us for miles before turning back and would even meet us weeks later as we turned the corner into Cumberland Bay. Gullible got so confident that he would sit on Tim's hand and allow his feathers to be touched by a tentative finger — but it was Gullible's undoing. Just before we left for a long September cruise he developed a sore right foot, barely able to put any weight on it. We thought there might be a splinter or foreign body causing this, so on the eve of departure Tim broke the bird's trust and quickly trapped and brought him below for examination. He lay almost paralyzed in Tim's hands, wide-eyed and heart thumping while I examined his foot with a magnifying glass but could see nothing and he was soon released, flying away totally confused. And Parkinson and Butterfly, who had witnessed the treachery and screamed in alarm, likewise avoided all further contact with *Curlew.*

We sailed. Gullible followed but would not land on *Curlew* as had been his habit, nor would he take any food on the wing from my hand. Two days later we came into Ocean Harbour, 20 miles sailing from Grytviken but only 10 as the gull flies. A second-year kelp gull flew round and round *Curlew* nervously, behavior different from that of any of the local gulls, who harried it and tried to drive it away. Eventually it landed exhausted and limped along the foreshore — with a sore right foot. It reappeared the next day, but then gales and blizzards intervened and we saw it no more.

During our fourth summer Parkinson and Butterfly brought two mewing fledglings to *Petrel* — but not to *Curlew.* A handsome bird in almost adult plumage took to sitting on the end of the boom. Gullible always had a poor memory.

IT IS MID-SEPTEMBER and I am working quietly in the Museum office. A loud crash followed by a scream penetrates the silence. There stands Skua in the snow with a rat almost half his size still struggling. But he holds it firmly in his bill. His wings are outstretched as if in triumph. Oh welcome home, Skua.

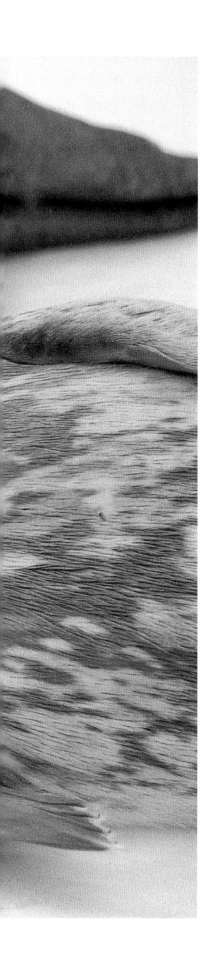

CHAPTER XII

The WILD SIDE

September 1995

P ITCH-DARK, BITTERLY COLD, a rocky cliff wall with overhanging snowbanks gleaming faintly, Cape pigeons chirring from the rocks and eerie, throaty Weddell seal noises echoing up through the water. It is calm now and the ice that had clogged Drygalski Fjord is half a mile astern. I try to find bottom with the leadline and suddenly there it is. . ."Yes, seven fathoms," Tim says. "Is it clear of kelp?" I use a powerful flash-light. "Okay, here." "Let go," he responds, and the anchor splashes down into Larsen Harbour. We've made it at last.

Ever since we first visited Larsen in the two previous summers and looked at the lovely adult Weddell seals that haul out daily on the shores, we wanted to be there for the breeding season. But pupping starts in August and finishes in September and no self-respecting, small, engineless boat should be down on the remote south coast in winter.

Curlew's stern lines were made fast to the cliff the next morning and Tim laid another anchor for safety. That way we knew she could withstand the fierce winds that whip down the narrow slit between 2,500-foot walls and we could sleep peacefully — come hell or high water. The mountains here are so close and so high that sitting on our settees in the cabin we could look straight up through the central hatch in the deck and admire them.

At last it was time to approach the moraine with the dinghy and lift it up onto the bank of snow that lay right to the water's edge. Now we could see close at hand the pups that I had already been watching impatiently through binoculars.

Beaming with anticipation, we crept slowly toward the beautiful little creatures with long, thick, ash blond fur and deep black shining eyes. Females with well-worn, end-of-season, splotchy coats looked old and tired by comparison to their newborn offspring whose cropped umbilical cords still hung red and moist from their bellies. Their thin bodies humped along like some jerky little caterpillar, not quite getting the hang of movement yet, but keen to try it. The mother would call them back and then, as they paid no attention at all, go up and physically pull them around with her teeth. Then the pups would roll about in the snow with their huge flippers flailing like rag dolls and gaze in astonishment at these disembodied parts of themselves that appeared to have a mind of their own.

Down by the shore a few pups were learning to swim, solicitous mothers watching their every move and keeping an eye out for any fur seal or other alien animals.

A much older pup was suckling and playing with its mother. It had already lost its natal hair and had a pristine silver patterned adult coat. Little mouth, complete with pearly teeth, snapped at its parent's whiskers and sniffed at her face, nuzzling affectionately and receiving the same profound care and attention back.

We watched all morning, drank from a hot flask and ate our sandwiches always with eyes glued on the enchanting animals. And then we watched some more, revelling in the opportunity that few, if any, people have had. South Georgia is the farthest north that Wed-

*Previous spread: A Weddell seal pup with mother. Weddells are the most southerly of all seals. **Opposite:** As we sail toward the south coast the dramatic peaks of the Salvesen Range dominate the scene.*

dells breed; they normally pup on the sea ice, where few scientists are able to reach them.

Weddells are the most southerly of seals and stay around Antarctica during the winter keeping breathing holes open in the ice by gnawing at it with their specially shaped teeth. Here they don't have to do that, although once, to my astonishment, I watched one neatly saw

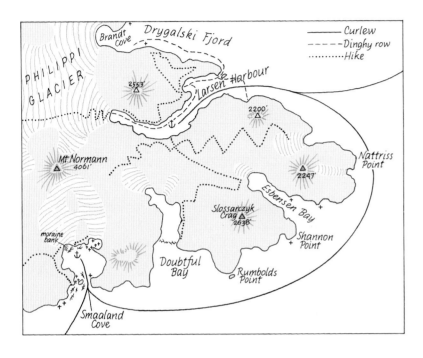

a head-sized circle in the ice off *Curlew*'s Grytviken berth and burst through with its flaring nostrils to breathe heavily for a while. I felt very privileged to have seen this. When Weddell seals die at around twenty years of age it is often because their teeth have become so blunt they can no longer keep their breathing holes open. At the other end of their bodies Weddells have beautiful tiny tails shaped like the spade in a deck of cards and edged with pale ivory hairs, far more elegant than the finger-like stubs of the elephant and fur seals we were more familiar with.

Another behavioral difference between Weddells here and farther south that we no-

LARSEN
HARBOUR AND
SMAALAND COVE

ticed was that the bulls would fight on the shoreline instead of in the sea — since here there was a beach to give them the option. Rearing up but much faster than the ponderous elephants and infinitely more stylized, they would go at each other viciously using teeth to bite and fore flippers outstretched both to balance themselves and to deliver disconcerting blows — then stop in mid-stroke, as it were, facing each other, poised motionless. They would fight again for maybe 10 seconds or so and then pause all over again just as though a referee's whistle had blown. One bull got his teeth into the other's flipper and, shaking his head, tore at it mercilessly. As we knew from their scars, they tend to bite down at the genital areas, which is, after all, quite logical. Guaranteed to cool a rival bull's ardor!

The resident bull trapped another bull at the water's edge and forced it up and onto the snow along with the females — quite the opposite of the elephants and fur seals, who drive their opponents back into the sea. No, this bull chased the vanquished one for several hun-

Curlew safely anchored in Larsen Harbour during summer. The mountains here are so close and so high that sitting in Curlew's *cabin we could look straight up through the hatch and admire them.*

dred feet along the snow, blood marking the trail, which we followed later, as far inland as was possible given the steep mountainside. What was more surprising to us was that there was no pausing for breath as there would have been with elephant seals.

Since the females will presumably mate in the water, as they do farther south, it makes sense for the bulls to corral their rivals up with the females who have pups, quite safe in the knowledge that they won't mate on land.

The most bizarre Weddell seal behavior came from our Grytviken resident bull. Maybe too young to go to Larsen and mix it with the mature bulls, he spent some of his time with the elephant seals. He once brought a protesting female to the slipway astern of *Curlew*, swimming close alongside her and preventing her from leaving until she beached herself right by his regular hauling-out place. Then he kept an eye on her for several hours until he fell asleep and she slid quietly away. Next we saw him in company with a mature bull, blowing bubbles into the elephant's face, nipping his hind flippers, and even climbing halfway up onto his back. Of course the bull was at least six times larger than the Weddell. At last he became so confident that he would pick on a bull, swim up to his head, and then flap him around the face with his dexterous flippers, a virtual boxing match that the elephant didn't take kindly to

*Above left: A Weddell pup only hours old, with its long natal hair. A slightly older pup (**above right**) rests with its mother after a swimming lesson. **Opposite left**: We saw many such endearing interactions between mothers and pups. A battle-weary dominant Weddell bull (**opposite right**) hauls out at low tide for a deep sleep.*

at all, complaining loudly. It was like some mismatched fight between flyweight and super-heavyweight. The Wed had the speed and nimble movements but we hoped he would never misjudge because the ellie's weight and massive teeth could have mangled our lovely friend.

WHILE WE WERE IN LARSEN WE PLANNED TO GO UP THE PHILIPPI GLACIER at the end of the inlet and ski over the great snow avenue to the west coast. Last summer we had climbed up the steep face of the glacier with crampons and ice axes. Later we talked to Tony Bomford, the surveyor who had helped make the first and only detailed maps of South Georgia from surveys spanning 1951–57, the same ones still in use. He assured us that back then it had been absolutely impossible to descend the snout of the glacier and the group of surveyors had to turn back and make a difficult descent into Brandt Cove by another route. It shows how South Georgia's glaciers are always changing, mostly now receding, and altering the possibilities of routes. This generally makes things more difficult as they pull away from the surrounding rocks leaving impassable chasms or bergschrunds. But in this case we had been lucky and the climb had eased up.

At the top, 1,000 feet up, we changed to skis and were soon elatedly speeding across virgin snowfield edged by hauntingly beautiful and lofty peaks. Big, rolling gray clouds would occasionally let sunbeams burst between them and spokes of white light radiated down from the heavens. To our right lay Brandt Cove, blue glaciers deeply crevassed and now unapproachable. The mountains to our left were fractured where they thrust upward another 3,000 feet from the great, smooth, inviting avenue.

One moment Tim was skiing along in great style ahead of me and then suddenly he disappeared. It took a second or two for me to realize that he gone into a crevasse, and I threw myself to a desperate stop. Creeping toward the treacherous split I was relieved to see the top of his head. Kneeling close, and praying that my little patch of safe snow would not disappear as well, I heaved as hard as I could on the shoulder straps of his big backpack. He used elbows and ski edges to work his way upward until he could get an arm over the top. He had time to look down and see deep, deep blue, and quite frankly it scared us witless. We were exceedingly lucky. The fissure was sufficiently narrow that his skis jammed and he only fell a few feet so that our combined efforts — mostly his adrenaline, I think — brought him out in less than a minute. But what a desperate minute.

Although we had roped up for the climb up the glacier, knowing that there would be a few crevasses there, we had misjudged the terrain up on the innocent-looking snowfield and had gaily abandoned the rope and crampons for skis, feeling that the 2 feet or more of snow

would be sufficient to bridge any rogue crevasses, whose existence we had seriously doubted anyway. Because we were skiing neither of us had ice axes ready to dig in for an anchor point, so we both were at high risk for some minutes and did not dare to admit our folly to anyone for a long time.

Added to that shock, when, several hours later, we returned to the place where we had left the dinghy, a major rock fall had just cascaded down the slopes above the dinghy and we couldn't see it at first. If it had been crushed under those tons of rock we would never have been able to get back to *Curlew* at least half a mile away. It would have required a highly

We have made many memorable trips to Larsen Harbour in summer. **Opposite:** *A pair of Antarctic skuas survey their territory and look toward the head of Drygalski Fjord.* **Above:** *Pauline surveys Williams Cove, a part of the harbor just off of Drygalski Fjord, with its sheer cliffs, one of South Georgia's most spectacular sights.*

technical rock climb for which we had neither equipment nor experience. Forget swimming — we couldn't have survived for long immersed in that icy water. Our remoteness in Larsen was complete. It is too narrow an inlet for any of the ships to enter and years can go by without another yacht visiting, so we could not have hoped for any help or rescue.

And now, in September, a combination of unappealingly windy weather followed by a premature thaw put us off repeating the adventure and I must admit I was secretly relieved.

For a long time we doubted whether we could complete the circuit around South Georgia with the formidable reputation of the wild west shores. Only four yachts had previously sailed here and all had resorted to their engines. In bad weather the Antarctic Ocean's huge southwesterly swells batter this coast relentlessly with little or no shelter to be found. Reading Shackleton's and Worsley's accounts was more than enough to sow very large seeds of doubt in my mind as to the wisdom of pushing our luck any further. . .and yet one particular photograph taken by Gerry Clarke of the tiny New Zealand "research vessel" *Totorore* and used on the cover of his book *The Totorore Voyage* showed a coastline even lovelier and more soul stirring than any we could have ever conceived.

During the summer of 1993–94 we spent a week in Smaaland Cove 5 miles from the aptly named Cape Disappointment on the southwest tip of the island. Captain Cook named it because it proved South Georgia was an island and not a projection of "Terra Australis Incognito," which existed only in theory but for which he was searching. For us the horrendous weather that blew around this even more isolated equivalent of Cape Horn was ample reason for the "disappointment" because we had hoped to reach the west coast from here.

Smaaland itself was perhaps the most spectacular anchorage *Curlew* has ever set trepidant keel into. A deep, circular bowl barred from the sea by an island, it is backed by Mount Normann, which climbs almost vertically as a sheer wall of ice to over 4,000 feet. The lower few hundred feet of ice is constantly calving large chunks of brash. To another direction lies a massive square-topped piton of over 2,000 feet while twin peaks of equal height grace the far side of the bay. On a good day it was absolutely outstanding — but there was only one good day in that week and the others varied from awful to appalling. On that one blessed day we climbed out of the cove and traversed across snow and scree between deeply crevassed glaciers, expansive snowfields, and impossible pinnacles to gaze upon the twin

---

Winter, just off Cape Disappointment, with the peaks of the Salvesen Range in all their glory.
If you think Cape Horn is a spectacular and wild place, you haven't been
to the southern tip of South Georgia.

peaks of Cape Disappointment and the ocean beyond. "It's not the end of the world, quite, but you can see it from here," Tim trotted out the cliché.

Then there followed a succession of hurricane-force gales while Mount Normann appeared occasionally, moonlit through the swirling cloud like some great ermine-clad monster pouring down his wrath upon his hapless mortals. We hung on to the moraine barrier with four anchors and the skin of our teeth as *Curlew* was being rocked and buffeted by almost constant icefalls. When we eventually scudded out with only a scrap of sail set, it was with gratitude that we had escaped in one piece. We knew that Jérôme had been forced to abandon all his anchor tackle there and *Damien II* only survived because of her powerful engine.

Above: Smaaland Cove in summer. It is perhaps the most extraordinary anchorage Curlew *has ever entered.*

Opposite: Pauline scrambles up the scree slope beside Mount Normann's very active 4,000-foot glacier.

T HE NEXT TIME WE ATTEMPTED THE WEST COAST, in the summer of 1994–95, it
was from the north, leaving Bird Island in fair weather. It fell calm overnight and
Curlew slipped along slowly with just enough speed to keep her pointing in the
right direction. By dawn we were passing inside the Hauge Reef, which has many large rocks
with tussocky tops, perhaps even big enough to be called small islands — as well as roughly
charted underwater dangers. Studying the chart we were amused by Mislaid Rock and rather
more chastened by Horror Rock. Beyond lay the elusive Annenkov Island. Angry yellow
light broke around the southern end of the island and briefly showed a spectacularly white
and glaciated coast with hardly a sign of tussock grass or the gentler, sloping ground that re-
lieves parts of the east coast. Somewhere up in the swirling cloud and icy buttresses was the
summit of Mount Paget. This was the side from which it had first been climbed, but it certainly didn't look any easier to us and the coast was infinitely wilder.

Diving petrels erupted out of the water ahead of *Curlew* and whirred along with their short wings for all the world like oversized bumblebees. Along with their Northern Hemisphere equivalents, the auks and guillemots, these little birds have the ability to fly above or below the waves as they choose. Ahead lay a possible safe anchorage that we had asked Jérôme about, but he had been rather vague. He also thought the way into the inner bay might have been too shallow for us. We found the outer bay where *Curlew* would have been dangerously exposed and then I tried to find a way in, with the dinghy and leadline, over a moraine barrier. Everywhere I looked it seemed too shallow for *Curlew*, whereas the specially designed *Damien II* could have lifted her keel hydraulically to slip over it. The weather was worsening rapidly and we were beginning to feel trapped and very vulnerable. "We'd better get out of here," called Tim, who was sailing *Curlew* in tight circles while he waited for me. We resigned ourselves and carried on putting reefs in the sails to contain the rising wind.

We checked out the only other possible anchorage on the southwest coast, Diaz Cove, and again decided it was unsafe in what was rapidly becoming a gale, and reluctantly beat back out to the entrance with the icy spray flying into our faces. By the time we reached Cape Disappointment we seemed to be in the same awful weather that had dogged us for so long at Smaaland. The ubiquitous williwaws swept down on us from the hoar-encrusted peaks of Cape Disappointment, 2,775 feet above. If you think Cape Horn is a spectacular and wild place, you haven't been to the southern tip of South Georgia. Tide rips steepened into fiercesome seas, and we gritted our teeth and rode with it — there was no alternative.

But there was exhilaration, too, as *Curlew* became as one with the ocean, no more significant than just a transient fleck of spray while our spirits were drawn into the wildness of the scene. We were no longer just observers but in some way belonged in that moment forever surrounded by primeval glory. This was a scene I had dreamed of at a latitude as far north as we were now south, and the dream and the reality were fused for a split second. Just as you sometimes dream of flying, my vision had been of surfing in these self-same wild seas with their unearthly, savage backdrop. But the dream had been one of total harmony and absence of fear because in some fantastical way I had become a whale and was not merely an interloper aboard a man-made boat.

Another squall rattled hail against our oilskin hoods and Tim struggled to the mast to pull down the small remaining area of mainsail and he cried out as a small, bottlenosed whale burst out from beneath our bow wave.

Curlew *moored to a cliff in Larsen Harbour. A promontory shelters her from the worst of the icy winds that blast down the narrow inlet from the Philippi glacier.*

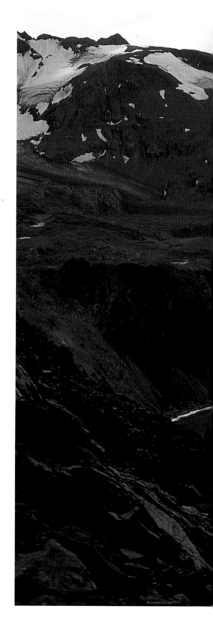

CHAPTER XIII

A SHIMMER

of ICE

October 1995

E'D BETTER GET OUT OF HERE at first

light." We lay in bed listening to the anchor chain rumbling

across a rocky bottom as *Curlew* was having a restless night. She

strained at her anchor with a choppy sea rolling into a small,

unnamed bay on the south coast, soon to be officially named

Damien Bay by the government.

There were rocks on either side of the entrance so we didn't want to beat out in the darkness but tied in the reef points to shorten the mainsail and snugged the little cutter down, hoping that the weather wouldn't worsen before dawn. A powerful engine could have taken us out of the bay on a straight, safe course, but we had managed this far. . . .

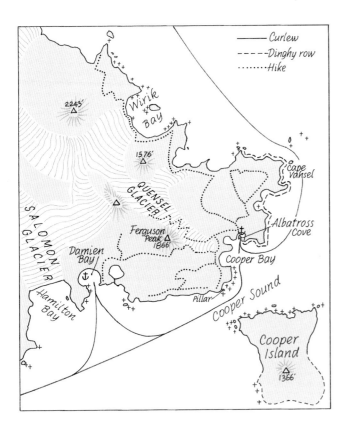

COOPER SOUND

It was another of those wild-looking mornings with harsh light reflecting off the sea and torn clouds spinning past the lurid mountain summits. The seas got much worse as we reached Cooper Sound, where the strong contrary current turned every wave into a hurdle for *Curlew* to climb. "This is silly, we're shaking the poor old girl to bits and getting nowhere." Tim considered turning back but Damien Bay offered no sanctuary and it would be a long slog against the wind into Larsen Harbour. Penguins plopped out of the steep seas occasionally and even they didn't look quite as masterful of their element as usual.

Almost without warning we were enveloped in fog. It had been sitting on the high ground of Cooper Island and a band of it lay far away on the horizon to the southwest, but the speed with which it arrived barely gave us time to take compass bearings. Since *Curlew* was still being swept with the current these wouldn't be useful for long. Suddenly the situation had become dangerous. Now it was too late to turn around so we had to keep creeping along with eyes straining for the first sign of breaking reef, only too well camouflaged amid the breaking seas. We blessed our familiarity with the coastline — because the chart certainly didn't have enough detail to help. After a very uneasy sail the mist cleared slightly to reveal a familiar pinnacle rock and we knew that the most dangerous reef would soon be lying across our track, but now that we had our bearings once more we could avoid it.

Previous spread: The rugged southeast coast with Iris Bay in the distance. Wirik Bay is past the waterfall in the middle distance. With care it is possible to scramble from Cooper Bay all the way to a lookout over Iris Bay. After a frightening stretch of rough seas and sudden fogs along a reef-strewn coast, we slid safely into tiny Albatross Cove in Cooper Sound, our favorite anchorage. Opposite: In the hills above Albatross Cove there are dozens of colonies of gentoo penguins. Raising two chicks, both with bulging crops, indicates that it has been a bumper summer.

And then just as suddenly as it had closed in on us the fog lifted and *Curlew* sailed into the sunlight and calm seas. Hell turned into heaven as she glided gently toward the tiny, rock-girded Albatross Cove and with the help of an oar slid into safety with only a few inches under her keel. Jérôme and Sally call it "Albatross Cove" because Niall Rankin's lifeboat *Albatross* was the first boat to use this anchorage in 1947 and he wrote about it in his book *Antarctic Isle*. It is too small to justify an official name — too small in fact to be much more than a nonchalant squiggle of the cartographer's hand.

It was the first week of October and *Curlew* was just 10 miles from Cape Disappointment. We had poked the bowsprit into Smaaland Cove only to find it completely full of ice, and a considerable iceberg had somehow fit through the entrance and grounded close to where we would have anchored. Despite the rough sail into Albatross Cove the big Southern Ocean swell had been unnaturally absent — we didn't question it but counted our blessings. There was more floating ice about than we had seen for a few years but nothing could touch

us here, we thought, and skied up among the pink-stained hilltops, home to dozens of colonies of gentoo penguins laying claim to their favorite spots and displaying and mating.

Each morning shortly after dawn they left their hilly lookouts and struggled down the slippery snow slopes to the sea to find krill and fish. The richness of the pink stains told us that the krill were abundant and the birds were back by lunchtime, replete. Everything pointed to a successful breeding season. Sitting in the sun beyond the black sand beach it was lovely to watch wave after wave of fat, well-fed penguins burst out of the breakers. Soon they would stand erect, bray triumphantly with their scarlet beaks thrust skyward and satiny chests heaving, preen, and then start their long trudge inland. And back up in the hills the

*Opposite: Gentoo penguins burst out of the surf in early October at the beginning of their breeding season. Many of the world's gentoos breed here in South Georgia. **Above:** Albatross Cove in summer, ringed with lush tussock grass.*

snow was melting around the tussocky summits and nest building was in full swing. Tim couldn't resist helping one trusting bird by passing it handfuls of grass. This sped up the process to produce a splendid nest. Quite an improvement on the stones and macabre bones that penguins use when there is no tussock.

A large part of the world's gentoo population lives in South Georgia. There are little colonies all over but seldom in larger groups than a few hundred pairs. Their bright red bills and salmon-colored feet contrast with the *de rigueur* black-and-white penguin livery and a broad unbroken white stripe tapers from eye to crown like a nurse's headdress. And the character that they exude is one of solemn, solicitous good nature, a little nervous perhaps if anything moves quickly, but "gentle gentoos" is quite appropriate.

We had always been told that when the gentoo fledglings finally swim away from their colonies in late summer their bond is broken with the parents and they become part of the large amorphous mass that porpoises its way out to sea to feed. But we once witnessed a most endearing and poignant meeting when two penguins emerged onto opposite ends of a stretch of beach at least 5 miles from the nearest colony. Quite literally they ran down the beach toward each other "with open arms," billing ecstatically for several minutes and then swimming away together into the dusk. Oh dear, Tim does not call me Anthropomorphic Annie for nothing! But we did notice that one had the new, pristine coat of a youngster whereas the other was obviously sun-bleached to a tired gray and in dire need of a refreshing molt. Surely a parent and erstwhile chick?

We skied to the top of the Quensel glacier and overlooked the east coast as far as Royal Bay. Then we telemarked down for three-quarters of an hour of serpentine twisting and turning, getting into a rhythm that was sheer bliss until our muscles began to ache. Then we stopped to exchange rapturous comments on the snow, the view, the skiing, and the wonderful world we inhabited.

The next day we went looking for more excitements and found one that capped them all. Skiing to a ridge on the south coast this time, Tim continued herringboning upward with more dedication and energy than I could muster so I paused for breath looking out toward Cooper Island and Cape Disappointment. The horizon was looking very pale. Was it a trick of the light? The old brain ticked slowly away as I climbed another hundred feet or so. Tim's trailblazing had been temporarily thwarted by an avalanche-prone slope and he was consid-

The northernmost colonies of chinstrap penguins in the world are found just west of Cooper Bay and on Cooper Island. Two kelp gulls stand atop the stack.

ering a new approach. So I got out the binoculars. Yes. There it was from horizon to horizon, white, solid, uncompromising, incredibly dangerous, and incredibly exciting. The pack ice had come to South Georgia from the deeper south. I passed the binoculars to Tim without comment. We sat down. "How much food and kerosene do we have left?" he questioned, at last. "So that's why the sea has been so flat lately. The ice has completely damped down the swell."

The gale-force winds blowing straight through the tiny channel into Albatross Cove meant it was virtually impossible to leave under sail. Besides, we were having such a lovely time it seemed a pity to cut our adventure short. The proximity of the pack was so exciting that one part of us was fascinated to see what was going to happen. *Curlew* should be safe in

A light-mantled sooty albatross has a commanding view of Cooper Bay and Albatross Cove. Another yacht, English Rose IV, *is sharing the cove with us.*

the tiny cove, we hoped, because it was so shallow and reef-strewn at the entrance that although the ice could enter it would be fragmented and not able to build up any pressure. Perhaps she might even be safer here than back in Grytviken if the pack ice was to extend far north and wrap around to enclose the whole east coast.

So we decided to wait and watch and went skiing daily to keep an eye on the jumbled white ice front. It grew significantly closer over four days and we could see the huge tabular bergs ensnared in the solid pack as it streamed toward the island. Millions, billions of tons of ice moving relentlessly, inexorably toward a slow death in the melting zones.

Then the barometer fell, the wind reached screaming point once more, and the current must have swirled too, for almost to our regret the ice was driven past Cooper Island and never made it into Cooper Sound or even close enough to photograph it effectively. Eventually it dispersed almost entirely and when Curlew did wriggle out of the narrow space between reefs and into the sound there were only a few small icebergs with attendant skeins of brash scattered along the coast ahead of us.

But at Bird Island their sound had been completely full of ice, so much so that they said it would almost have been possible to cross, floe hopping to the mainland. Jérôme arrived a week later, ready to start an elephant seal count for the whole island, and he could not at first force Damien II into the cove because of the residual ice clogging it. For big, steel Damien it was not really a problem but if little, wooden Curlew had been there, as she had been the previous year at that time. . . . Later, as Jérôme surveyed the west coast, counting elephants on every beach, he found that all kelp and marine growth had been scoured clean from the rocks by the insistent grating of the ice. This is a phenomenon only recorded twice before in this century so we were very privileged to witness it. Just when you think you've seen everything, South Georgia springs a new surprise.

As Curlew SAILED IN THE DARK THROUGH MIST AND ICE on her way home our eyes strained myopically to pick out the dangers before they picked us out. Again the weather had changed without allowing us time to find shelter. The remnants of the pack ice lay strewn all over the coast, with plenty of room to sail between dangers given good visibility but dangerous at night. Suddenly the full moon rose above the bank of cloud and the ice reflected back at us as though painted with fluorescence. A light breeze gave Curlew just the impetus she needed and we headed for the coast where Mount Paget and its cohorts were white silhouettes against the velvet sky, now pinpricked with pulsating winter stars. Tim came on deck to relieve me but it was too good a sight to leave and we stayed cuddled up together in the cold, entranced.

"Let's go into Ocean Harbour and get some sleep." Tim headed *Curlew* in while I went below to get a warm drink for us both. I felt the boat tack suddenly as a stream of brash ice seemingly without end lay across our route. But deep into Hound Bay we slipped around it and picked out the line of sharp rocks that forms Tijuca Point and the entrance to Ocean Harbour. The clear sky made it very cold again and *Curlew* began to push through newly forming ice. The breeze dropped close to the coast and she had barely enough power to keep breaking the thin but solid sheet as it scrunched past the hull noisily, resisting her efforts. Infinitely slowly we gained a little distance and the dramatic, dark hulk of *Bayard* began to show up against the moonlit hillsides. The sounds of surf at the entrance gave way to the roars and protests of the elephant seal colonies newly pupping on the beach at the head of the bay. Another paradise to savor for a few more days until duty returned us to Grytviken for the beginning of our fourth summer.

Tied up again we didn't bother with the protective ice lines in our haste to ski to the point to see Pat and Sarah and collect our mail. The post office and the welcome were warm. We raised a glass or two and bubbled over with our news and stories of the past six weeks. Pat and Sarah tried hard not to be envious, restricted as they were without a boat and with a much more constraining job. We were very aware of our blessings.

Later that night we woke to the sickeningly familiar sound of crackling, fizzing, thawing iceberg. Rushing on deck nearly naked, we found a substantial bergy bit about to hit us. Tim swung onto the end of the bowsprit in a flash and started fending off the ice with his bare feet, yelling for me to give him the boathook. It was still lashed down from sailing and the lashings were now frozen solid so I pummeled frantically at them to undo the knots. Tim tried to hold off the ice with the boathook while I went below to put on more clothes. It was snowing and bitterly cold. A moderate easterly wind was bouncing the boat up and down, threatening to break off her bowsprit if it hit the bergy bit with any momentum. I was already chilled to the bone and shaking so much I couldn't get dressed properly, and the lighter was damp and wouldn't light the oil lamp. Still wet and not really adequately clad I relieved a frozen Tim but then accidentally kicked over the chimney, which belched soot and toxic fumes into the dark cabin. Tim exploded back out spluttering in disgust.

Eventually we realized that the bergy bit had gone aground just ahead of *Curlew* — it

A still, clear pool of South Georgia wine, perhaps the purest water on earth.
The Salvesen Range lies beyond, with Douglas Crag (5,478 feet) and
Mount Carse (7,649 feet) with its mantle of clouds.

was larger than her and many times her weight. Another few inches closer and it would have jammed one of its spurs underneath the gyrating bowsprit and we would have been in big trouble. As the tide rose and the bergy bit was again afloat, we had to keep pressure on to prevent it from working its way in further on top of us. I expected the boathook to splinter at any moment as it bent and buckled and skidded across the rock-hard surface, but it did not break, and we were able to push the menace away an inch at a time until it lay off to the side and the danger diminished. Then sometime in the long night it rolled over with a huge commotion, narrowly missing us again. What a neighbor to cohabit a confined space. At dawn the wind came up from the west and it blew back out to sea and the ordeal was over. Tim replaced the broken chimney, I cleaned up the sooty chaos, we had some breakfast and crawled thankfully back to bed.

A few weeks later the first cruise liner of the season came into the cove and tied up at the ramshackle jetty in front of the museum. Fresh snow had fallen and the group of red-coated tourists stumbled knee-deep after Tim as he skied ahead of them out to Shackleton's grave by way of the elephant seal colony. "It would be best to keep in my tracks," he cautioned, avoiding holes in the jetties, obstacles hidden under the snow, and the thinly disguised elephant seal wallows.

These erstwhile cosseted passengers had been viewing the hostile environment through sanitizing, insulating plate glass and now they were face-to-face with a birthing elephant seal. Perhaps this is what they were secretly hoping for — hands-on experience, the biting blizzard in their faces, the pungent animal smell, even the creeping icy discomfort as the chill water found its way between carefully layered clothing.

Later that evening the culture shock was reversed as we were invited for dinner on board the ship. Beyond the gangway, as the outer door closed behind us, was a calm, warm, carpeted world with soft music, perfumed air, and gentle chatter. Beautiful stewardesses with manicured hands smilingly offered us drinks. There were tantalizingly short meetings with kindred spirits and fascinating people from another world. They are all bound together by the deep desire to experience — in the only way possible — these remote reaches of the earth and the paradoxically accessible wildlife.

Sampling our way through a succession of gastronomical delights, glasses kept topped to overflowing, it was easy to become loquacious from the constant stream of questions. Occasionally we caught each other's eyes to remind ourselves of the other world outside.

A cold, clear sunrise at the beginning of another beautiful South Georgian day.

"But surely you don't stay here all winter, do you? Isn't it very boring?" "Not exactly," said Tim, grinning sideways at me, as we mentally tallied the museum work, the almost-finished wooden rowing boat Tim had made, the whalebone chess set he was carving, the writing, photography, and wildlife watching, the sailing, skiing, and climbing.

"What do you miss most?" We had to think about that for a while because there is very little we really yearn for. Then, simultaneously: "Trees," Tim said. "Fruit," said I.

One of the passengers said, "I wanted to give you this," and he passed us a hand-scripted "certificate" on the ship's notepaper with the following quote:

The Storm increases, the Sea runs high, the Snow makes the Air thick, we cannot see ten yards before us, happily the wind is off shore. If a Captain, some Officers & a Crew were convicted of some heinous crimes, they ought to be sent by way of punishment to these inhospitable cursed Regions, for to explore & survey them. The very thought to live here a year fills the whole Soul with horror & despair. God! what miserable wretches must they be, that live here in these terrible Climates. Clarity lets me hope, that human nature was never thought so low by his Maker, as to be doomed to lead or rather languish out so miserable a life.
— Johann Reinhold Forster,
naturalist aboard Captain Cook's *Resolution* in 1775, writing about South Georgia

Everyone laughed at the contrast in attitudes and views between then and now. And we noted that the certificate was addressed: "To the luckiest people on earth."
Like Cinderellas leaving the ball we negotiated the gangway before midnight to find a

*Above: Clearing winter skies above Ocean Harbour. We slipped into this safe haven under pulsating winter stars on our way back to Grytviken. **Opposite:** Infinitely slowly we gained a little distance and the dramatic, dark bulk of Bayard began to show up against the hillsides.*

clear night, almost warm by South Georgian standards. The liner looked like a spaceship, its tiered rows of lights even more dazzling against the deepest dark that is Grytviken's norm. There was the hum of generators and engines as the red, portside navigation light and ice searchlight were switched on and the crew prepared to take the passengers toward their next experience.

WE STOOD ARM-IN-ARM on the dock ready to help let go the mooring lines. A mass of pink was boiling to the water surface in whale-sized mouthfuls. Krill. Right in the cove and here by the ton. This was the fuel for the Antarctic powerhouse — a sign that all was well in this part of the world. Tim dipped his hand into the water and looked at the tiny shrimp-like creatures. "Looks like it's going to be another brilliant summer."

The ship and her lights departed and the bay became silent and dark again. The stars were no longer eclipsed and we could pick out the familiar constellations. There, sharing the euphoria of the moment, was Orion, the hunter of the north, caught in mid-cartwheel, as if from peak to peak across the northern valley.

And as we skied the couple of minutes home to a cozy *Curlew*, the Southern Cross was flying like a kite from her masthead. The stars told us that we stood between two hemispheres, two seasons, and judging from the evening among the cruise ship glitterati, two worlds.

The choice is ours but we know that the reality lies here. In three weeks time the people on the ship would be back home, their trips just a rich memory. A once-in-a-lifetime flash. Our own experience is enriched as the years go by and glows like the stars — as brilliant, as intangible, and just as spellbinding.

CHAPTER XIV

A CLEAN PAIR
of HEELS

NONE OF THIS STORY WOULD BE POSSIBLE

without *Curlew* and her charisma. For thirty years of our lives

her spirit has lifted the most prosaic days. Her timelessly ele-

gant lines always gladden our eyes as we row toward her. In 1998

she becomes a hundred years old and it is sad, but inevitable,

that none of her original builders or her first owner is left alive

to marvel at the miracle.

239

Frank Jose was born and bred in Falmouth in the west country of England. When just a boy he ran away to sea and sailed aboard a ship bound for Australia. The crew mutinied and he ran away again — this time into the bush. But he was caught, flogged, lost an eye, and then somehow managed to return home. After that he didn't leave his home waters again but became one of the Falmouth watermen who sailed the Falmouth quay punt fleet, the little boats that met the sailing ships far out at sea on their approach to Falmouth and offered their services as a supply boat for the duration of the visits. Glorified bum boats they might have been, but their seaworthiness became legend.

Previous spread: Curlew *sails into Cumberland Bay, to be her home waters for the next five years and more. Tim and Pauline's early days aboard* Curlew, *cruising in Greece (left).* **Above:** Curlew, *Falmouth Quay Punt, circa 1900, working for her living.* **Opposite:** *Frank Jose aboard* Curlew. *He owned and worked her for 38 years between 1898 and 1936.*

Eventually Frank Jose went to local boatbuilders R. S. Burt and Sons and negotiated with them to build a vessel of his own for the princely sum of £80. She was to be 28 feet long and 9 feet wide, with a draft of 6 feet, all fairly standard dimensions. But he also asked for all sorts of innovations, such as a much more cutaway forefoot, finer, sharper hull sections, and a rounded profile to the bottom of her keel, which was to be cast of iron and weigh over 4 tons. Putting all the ballast on the outside of the boat was definitely seen as radical in those days, and the skeptics on the waterfront shook their heads.

Above: Pauline and Curlew *in 1968 on their first cruise, around Malta and Gozo. Notice the boxy raised cabin, removed in Australia in 1979 after an accident with a fishing boat nearly shattered* Curlew.
Opposite: In 1985, with a new cold molded overlay on her hull and a new suit of sails, Curlew *was unbeatable.*

But when *Curlew* was launched and raced in the fiercely competitive summer regattas those same skeptics were lining up to sail with her as she showed a clean pair of heels and a foaming wake to the opposition.

The builders worked from a half model, a wooden carving of one entire side of the projected boat that could be whittled and modified to suit the owner's particular whim. No paper plans for these artistic men. In Falmouth the boatbuilding heritage was as rich as the pitch in the pine stacked up in the boatshed.

Curlew's framing was built from offcuts of English oak left over from the building of much larger ships, the West Country schooners. This timber was kept in the pickling ponds, where it lay immersed in salt water that would help to preserve it over the years. Then Frank Jose would lovingly paint the newly shaped timbers of his boat with a mixture of paraffin and linseed oil in the evenings when the shipwright and his apprentice had

laid down their tools and gone home. Her planking was finest imported pitch pine (American long-leafed yellow pine). This was often referred to as poor man's teak — for *Curlew* was, after all, just a working boat that had to justify her cost by earning a living. Accordingly she was fastened with iron spikes, not the bronze screws or copper rivets of the yachts of her time. A foredeck and narrow side-decks were added with coamings to keep the water from spilling into the otherwise open boat. The wood for her rudder was twisty, interlocking grain elm to withstand the strains of steering in the Western Approaches, where the Atlantic rolls around the western tip of England and gradually loses its violence.

The quay punts were rigged as yawls — that is, with a short second mast right aft — so as to spread the sail area as low as possible. This was because they would frequently have to sail in alongside a sailing ship and not get entangled in the ship's overhanging yards. Occasionally *Curlew* would be asked to do this even before the ship came to anchor and was still plowing along under sail, calling for Frank Jose's fine judgment and seamanship.

That she would be gaff-rigged was not questioned in those days since it would provide all the power a heavy boat needed to carry out her tasks efficiently. On a boat like *Curlew*, the more modern triangular Bermudan mainsail would be cripplingly small unless her mast was enormously tall to compensate. It was also a very simple, basic rig with no newfangled, costly, and untrustworthy yachty fittings.

Frank Jose loved his little boat and the freedom she gave him from the drudgery of working long hours, cap in hand, in some soul-destroying factory or office. He managed to make a living from 1898 until 1936, when he was getting on in years and the sailing ship trade had dwindled to nothing. Most of the punts had been superseded by engined launches which serviced the steam- and diesel-powered ships that called for their services by radio. This relegated the derring-do of the old puntmen into history while their boats were consigned to rot in creeks or were sold for conversion into gentlemen's yachts.

Curlew lasted longer than most because Frank eeked out his living by taking the holiday-making gentry on fishing trips and picnics across the bay. It was a long journey around the edges of the various inlets by horse and trap and later by car, but a glittering short sail across the inviting waters of the Fal River.

From the top story of their terraced house high on the cobblestoned hill above the town his daughter-in-law Brenda would watch out for *Curlew*'s unmistakable shape running back into the harbor. Then she would call to Frank's wife that Dad would be home in half an hour and they would speculate on what delicacies might be left over from the gentry's wicker hampers. Some of the leading families of the day trailed their fingers into the water from *Curlew*'s narrow decks, including the Cadburys, the Wills, and the Krafts. "One of nature's gentlemen," they called Frank Jose and then booked *Curlew* again for the following year.

But all the good times ended and *Curlew* was eventually and sadly sold. At first she stayed in Falmouth where a retired army man had an engine installed, then she went to the Sea

Opposite: *Tim and Pauline sailing in the Eggemoggin Reach, Maine.*
Above: *A good breeze in the Derwent River near Hobart, Tasmania, 1981.*
With her newly built flush deck Curlew *foams along at hull speed: 8 knots.*

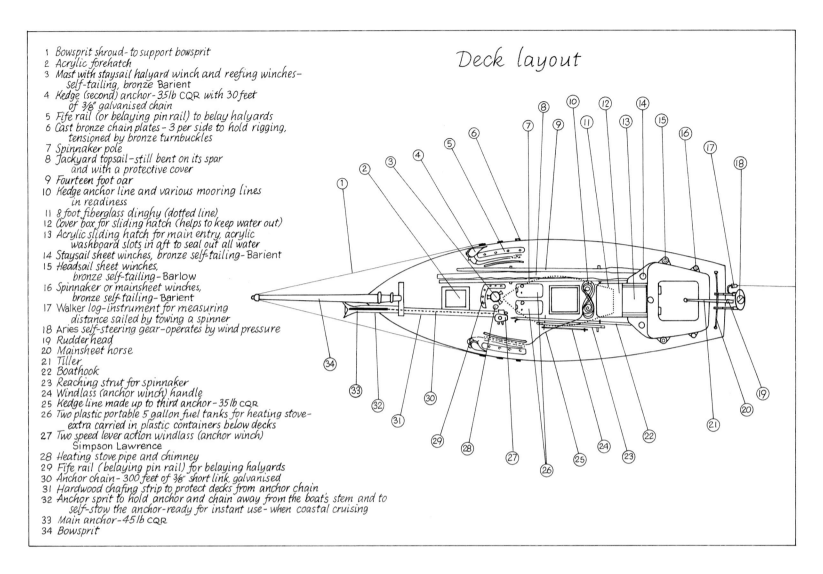

Deck layout

1 Bowsprit shroud - to support bowsprit
2 Acrylic forehatch
3 Mast with staysail halyard winch and reefing winches - self-tailing, bronze Barient
4 Kedge (second) anchor - 35 lb CQR with 30 feet of 3/8" galvanised chain
5 Fife rail (or belaying pin rail) to belay halyards
6 Cast bronze chain plates - 3 per side to hold rigging, tensioned by bronze turnbuckles
7 Spinnaker pole
8 Jackyard topsail - still bent on its spar and with a protective cover
9 Fourteen foot oar
10 Kedge anchor line and various mooring lines in readiness
11 8 foot fiberglass dinghy (dotted line)
12 Cover box for sliding hatch (helps to keep water out)
13 Acrylic sliding hatch for main entry, acrylic washboard slots in aft to seal out all water
14 Staysail sheet winches, bronze self-tailing - Barient
15 Headsail sheet winches, bronze self-tailing - Barlow
16 Spinnaker or mainsheet winches, bronze self-tailing - Barient
17 Walker log - instrument for measuring distance sailed by towing a spinner
18 Aries self-steering gear - operates by wind pressure
19 Rudder head
20 Mainsheet horse
21 Tiller
22 Boathook
23 Reaching strut for spinnaker
24 Windlass (anchor winch) handle
25 Kedge line made up to third anchor - 35 lb CQR
26 Two plastic portable 5 gallon fuel tanks for heating stove - extra carried in plastic containers below decks
27 Two speed lever action windlass (anchor winch) Simpson Lawrence
28 Heating stove pipe and chimney
29 Fife rail (belaying pin rail) for belaying halyards
30 Anchor chain - 300 feet of 3/8" short link, galvanised
31 Hardwood chafing strip to protect decks from anchor chain
32 Anchor sprit to hold anchor and chain away from the boat's stem and to self-stow the anchor - ready for instant use - when coastal cruising
33 Main anchor - 45 lb CQR
34 Bowsprit

Cadets at Penzance. During the war years she suffered badly when she chafed against a stone quay wall and eventually sank. Brought back to Falmouth, she was converted to a yacht with the addition of a dreadfully ugly, boxy cabin, a mahogany interior, and new spars. Later another owner motored her through the French canals to the Mediterranean and eventually she made her way to Malta, where she became a virtual derelict.

AND THAT IS WHERE WE FOUND HER IN 1967. She was a sorry sight with the rig cut down, lines festooned with weed, canvas sails disintegrating, paint peeling, a bilge full of leaked diesel, and overall a pervading smell of rot. But we ignored such "minor" details. Above all we could afford her £750 ($1,500 then) cost. The price of freedom, which even doubled as a home, was the same as that of a secondhand car.

In these early days Tim and I were taking the first faltering steps to weld our relationship and then *Curlew* came along and gave us direction and purpose. In Tim's case, after an un-

Interior layout

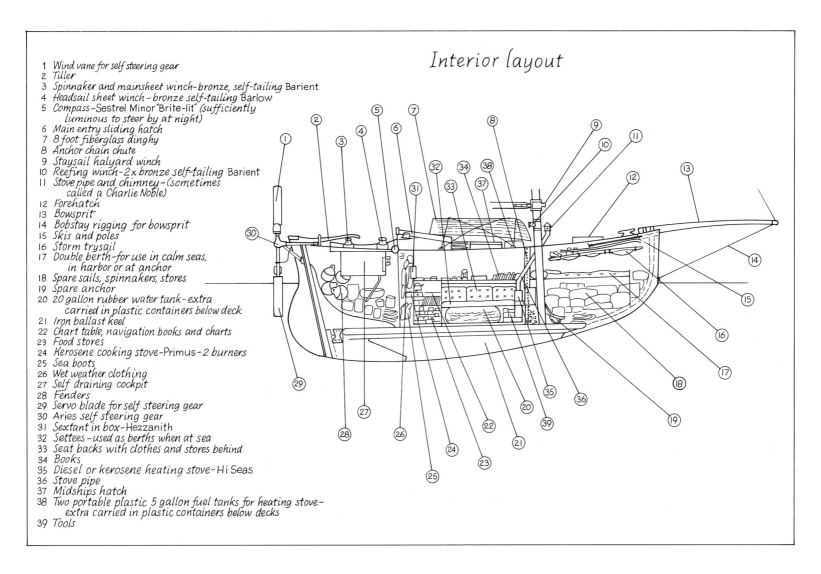

1 Wind vane for self steering gear
2 Tiller
3 Spinnaker and mainsheet winch-bronze, self-tailing Barient
4 Headsail sheet winch - bronze self-tailing Barlow
5 Compass-Sestrel Minor "Brite-lit" (sufficiently
        luminous to steer by at night)
6 Main entry sliding hatch
7 8 foot fiberglass dinghy
8 Anchor chain chute
9 Staysail halyard winch
10 Reefing winch-2x bronze self-tailing Barient
11 Stove pipe and chimney-(sometimes
        called a Charlie Noble)
12 Forehatch
13 Bowsprit
14 Bobstay rigging for bowsprit
15 Skis and poles
16 Storm trysail
17 Double berth-for use in calm seas,
        in harbor or at anchor
18 Spare sails, spinnakers, stores
19 Spare anchor
20 20 gallon rubber water tank-extra
        carried in plastic containers below deck
21 Iron ballast keel
22 Chart table, navigation books and charts
23 Food stores
24 Kerosene cooking stove-Primus-2 burners
25 Sea boots
26 Wet weather clothing
27 Self draining cockpit
28 Fenders
29 Servo blade for self steering gear
30 Aries self steering gear
31 Sextant in box-Hezzanith
32 Settees - used as berths when at sea
33 Seat backs with clothes and stores behind
34 Books
35 Diesel or kerosene heating stove-Hi Seas
36 Stove pipe
37 Midships hatch
38 Two portable plastic 5 gallon fuel tanks for heating stove-
        extra carried in plastic containers below decks
39 Tools

happy and bruised childhood, this was a chance to take life in his own hands and create a haven of peace and security. Yet paradoxically this also meant escape from a mundane and messed-up world. He decided then that the boat and the lifestyle would require our total commitment, but he knew instinctively that *Curlew* would give us the greatest of rewards.

We bought new tan-colored sails, stainless-steel rigging wire, and more chain and bigger anchors, and lavished paint and preservatives on a boat that was rapidly repaying us by the sheer bliss of our first tentative sails along the summer-calm coast. The world would be our oyster and *Curlew* the pearl. Naively we dreamed, in those early days. But slowly the reality of the dreams crept up on us as we left on our first Mediterranean cruise to Corfu and the Ionian Islands, ancient lands whose very breezes were caught by history. *Curlew* glided from oleander-fringed anchorages and pine-scented bays to medieval, granite-walled harbors. Tim dived to spear fish and I learned to bake bread. Adventure and excitement were not just around the corner; they already surrounded us.

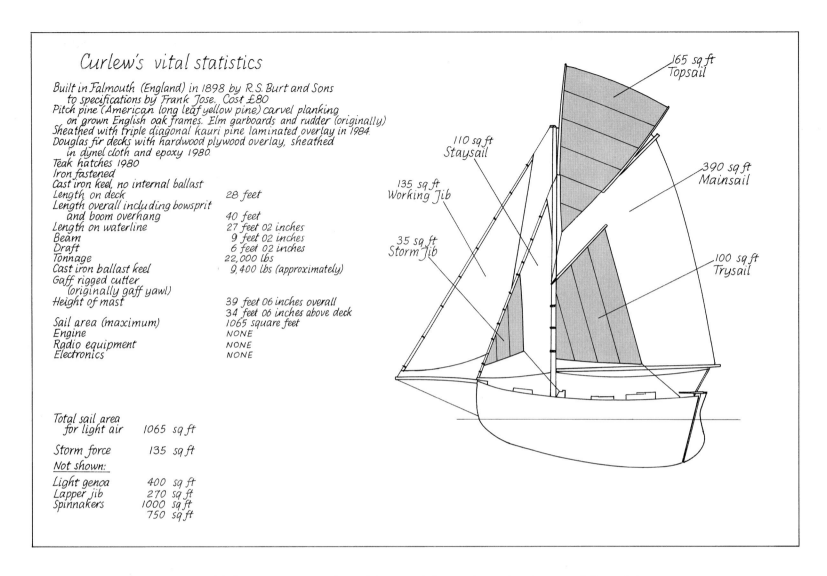

Curlew's vital statistics

Built in Falmouth (England) in 1898 by R.S. Burt and Sons
  to specifications by Frank Jose. Cost £80
Pitch pine (American long leaf yellow pine) carvel planking
  on grown English oak frames. Elm garboards and rudder (originally)
Sheathed with triple diagonal kauri pine laminated overlay in 1984.
Douglas fir decks with hardwood plywood overlay, sheathed
  in dynel cloth and epoxy 1980.
Teak hatches 1980
Iron fastened
Cast iron keel, no internal ballast

Length on deck	28 feet
Length overall including bowsprit and boom overhang	40 feet
Length on waterline	27 feet 02 inches
Beam	9 feet 02 inches
Draft	6 feet 02 inches
Tonnage	22,000 lbs
Cast iron ballast keel	9,400 lbs (approximately)

Gaff rigged cutter
  (originally gaff yawl)

Height of mast	39 feet 06 inches overall
	34 feet 06 inches above deck
Sail area (maximum)	1065 square feet
Engine	NONE
Radio equipment	NONE
Electronics	NONE

Total sail area for light air	1065	sq ft
Storm force	135	sq ft

Not shown:

Light genoa	400	sq ft
Lapper jib	270	sq ft
Spinnakers	1000	sq ft
	750	sq ft

Sail labels on diagram:
165 sq ft Topsail
110 sq ft Staysail
135 sq ft Working Jib
35 sq ft Storm Jib
390 sq ft Mainsail
100 sq ft Trysail

We sold the engine to a Maltese fisherman. The mechanical toilet soon followed the engine out of the boat, then the large gas oven was exchanged for a small kerosene Primus stove. Pooling our now meager resources we bought the essentials for crossing oceans. My jewelry went to help pay for an ancient secondhand sextant, a chronometer, and a new compass. We also bought an Aries self-steering gear, a wonderful contraption that virtually steered *Curlew* all around the world, deriving its power simply from the wind and the pressure of the sea running past us. Tim made many improvements, including a self-draining cockpit to drain water back into the sea rather than unhelpfully into the bilges, new rigging, and new spars. I struggled to learn navigation; then we both had to fathom out the finer points under way. "Just sail south and turn right when the butter melts" was the joking advice for finding the Caribbean. We could only afford margarine and it didn't melt! Somehow, though, we always managed to find the right islands.

At last *Curlew* was running downwind in the generous trade winds, speeding across the

Atlantic to Grenada in the lush Windward Islands. Our land-starved, ocean-adjusted senses could scarcely take in all the new impressions — the shining green foliage and the exotic smells of warm earth, tropical fruit, and spices, the muted sounds of a steel band reaching out across the water.

There was little money to spare — we had crossed the Atlantic with a £5 note — but Tim always managed to land a job at the crucial moment with his sailing and woodworking talents, and I did a host of small jobs to help keep bread on the table.

The gates of the Pacific Ocean opened as the last Panama Canal lock closed astern. A year in Hawaii, a year in Tahiti; whoever said dreams couldn't come true. A sailing ship-wreck on Suvarov Atoll disclosed gold nuggets shining on the deserted beach. When the wave action ceased to polish them in the sand, they slowly turned green — just broken sections of bronze fastenings. We didn't care. The real treasure was in spending three precious months there, living off the natural bounty of the sea and land.

We reached New Zealand, a tense, dawn landfall seen through salt-encrusted, weary eyes after a bitterly cold and nerve-racking struggle under storm canvas. The angry seas moderated, then became placid in the lee of an exquisitely beautiful "cloud-cuckoo-land." Mist in green valleys was enfolded by hills dotted with lollipop trees, like a child's story book illustration. *Curlew* had run a gauntlet to yet another enchanting world.

I T WAS NOW NINE YEARS SINCE *Curlew* had first set out from Malta but a myriad of valuable memories was her only cargo. Tim had long since decided that keeping the boat simple, uncluttered, and as light as possible would be the way to get maximum performance and enjoyment from her. This soon led to local yacht racing wherever we sailed, from New Zealand to Australia, Mauritius to South Africa, Brazil back to the Caribbean.

The racing bug bit deep and we saved enough money for some really good sails and suddenly *Curlew* was a threat to the locals. As our experience grew so did the list of trophies won, nearly all of which got returned to the relevant clubs, in keeping with the "uncluttered" image.

Hobart, Tasmania, was a good proving ground. Every windy weekend we "flogged the old tart around the buoys," as a crew member once said with grudging admiration. *Curlew* worked her way up through the divisions, hanging on to sail when squalls hit and laid the lighter, modern boats flat in the water. Then the old cutter's wake would be arrow straight, the tiller quivering gently amidships with fingertip steering. The bow wave would overlap the stem, the hull would be surrounded by flying white foam, and *Curlew* was pushed to the limit—and she loved it.

A major step in the gradual upgrading of our little vessel came in Australia in 1979 when we took off the boxy old cabin. It wasn't exactly planned but came about as the result of a near-catastrophic accident. A drunken fisherman drove his large vessel full astern into *Curlew* one night while we were at anchor. A loud roar of engines filled the cabin and *Curlew* was pushed downward under the water. We struggled desperately back to consciousness to escape from being trapped, rushing onto the deck a few seconds after the crash.

At first we feared our little vessel had been damaged beyond repair. Our anguish was extreme. We lay together the following night in abject misery, bodies rigid with grief, clinging to each other for comfort and solace. Then Tim decided that if he built a sleek new flush deck it would also add enormous strength and compensate for *Curlew*'s quite literally shattering experience. We began to look to a future once more. The standing headroom was sacrificed but we gained in aesthetics and improved working deck area. Belowdecks we removed the bulkheads so that there was an uninterrupted view from stem to stern, which helped to give an illusion of space. With no furniture above sitting shoulder height the craftsmanship of R. S. Burt and Sons could then be seen with the frames and planking exposed and varnished. And married happily to this nineteenth-century work are Tim's own repairs and new construction, especially the hanging knees, which are gracefully curved, hardwood brackets that tie in and support the new fir deck beams and decking.

There had been no insurance money — it would have been difficult if not impossible to obtain insurance for *Curlew* — and the fisherman had a convenient out because there were no witnesses to the accident who could prove our anchor light was still lit at the time of the impact. Yet it was a vivid lesson showing us how good can come out of bad and how this desperate situation actually put *Curlew* on the path to greater seaworthiness.

The second and more revolutionary transformation came about during our third visit to New Zealand in 1983–84. Because *Curlew*'s original fastenings were iron, they had, over such a long lifetime, corroded and affected the adjoining wood, causing what is known as "nail sickness." Other owners had hammered in a few extra nails with more enthusiasm than knowledge or accuracy, and we had completely refastened her in Hawaii in 1974. So there were also far more perforations in the planking than there ever should have been and we began to worry, thinking about the "postage-stamp syndrome," where you just tear along the dotted line. . .and the plank falls off!

The solution came from an article in *Wooden Boat* magazine and very soon we were laminating three new ⅛-inch layers of an excellent New Zealand timber, called kauri pine, over *Curlew*'s original hull planking. The whole operation took the two of us five months, working dawn to dusk. . .and then some. We lived in a small trailer adjoining the private boatshed that we were renting and, apart from a runaway bushfire that nearly destroyed the phoenix

before she could arise, it all went wonderfully well. When we relaunched in spring the hull was actually lighter since the old wood had dried out and then been impregnated with epoxy resin. It was even smoother than when new, tough enough to take the knocks, and able to be driven harder than ever before. This was to stand us in great stead for the future in high latitudes. More immediately, it made a big difference to the racing results.

Perhaps the culmination of our efforts came at the 1987 Antigua Week Regatta, which is quite an event on the international racing calendar. *Curlew* was easily the oldest entrant, the smallest, and the only one with the so-called obsolete gaff rig! "Jes watch dee batwing go,

In South Georgia ice begins to form around Curlew *in May. Whatever the season, she is our home; here Pauline has taken advantage of a bit of sunshine to hang the laundry. The net bag on the inner forestay holds reindeer meat out of the way of kelp gulls and rats.*

man. Ah got mah shirt on dat ole boat," called *Curlew's* West Indian fans. And she didn't disappoint them, winning the second-best performance overall and easily winning her class — and the competition included some very modern designs.

It was all so absurd seeing this anachronistic boat cleaning up the prizes that most people just threw their hands up and laughed. A few more curious ones would come and visit her soon after a race, often swimming across and having a look at her keel on the way. Of course, they just might have been looking for a propeller — or feeling beneath the lockers for a warm engine. We generally opened up the "engine box" and produced a cabbage or bottle of wine and confounded them with a smile!

But adventure lured us away from this slightly decadent and indulgent lifestyle in the tropics and back to the more exciting realities of a very cold winter frozen into the Passagassawaukeag River in Maine. Summer brought us otters, caribou, and our first icebergs off Newfoundland, and then puffins and glaciers in Northern Iceland. Eventually, by way of the west coasts of Scotland and Ireland, *Curlew* was bracing her sails against the wind for the beat back into Falmouth Harbour and at last came to anchor off the same quay that she had left so long before. Two days later she won all three trophies at the annual Falmouth Classics regatta.

Not long after that we had *Curlew* craned out onto an old quayside at the head of a creek above the town while we painted the underwater parts of her hull. A man was gazing up at her with more than a passing interest. We smiled at him and said hello.

"My name is Eric Jose." The slightly diffident Cornishman held out his hand to us. "It was my grandfather who had this boat built." We dropped tools and invited him aboard. "We used to think of *Curlew* as one of the family and always wondered what had happened to her." He was settled down in the cabin with a cup of coffee in his hand, the varnished planking sunlit behind his head, the same boards that his grandfather had so carefully preserved more than ninety years ago. "It is wonderful to see how well she looks," he told us. "Brenda, my mother, is still very hearty, and she has some old photographs of *Curlew* you might like to see. Would you care to come up to our place for dinner tonight?"

A fascinating evening was followed by a memorable sail when Eric Jose, who had never steered a sailing boat in his life, took *Curlew's* tiller in his tradesman's hands and steered her as instinctively as his grandfather must have done. Past the town, down to the Manacles, and toward the Lizard.

Soon, though, the luster of late summer wore off and we became horribly aware of the

Pauline hoists the staysail as Curlew *heads off into a promising day.*

crawling, grinding, polluting traffic, the commercialism and the crowds, the cynicism of a weary population coming to terms with recession. It was no longer the small, quaint, hard-working town of *Curlew*'s early days and we felt the time had come to sail again to remoter regions. We gave *Curlew* a thorough refit, again blessing her few and simple needs. At last we had our freedom again and the Atlantic swells were carrying our magic carpet gently on her way south.

S O HERE WE ARE — a long, winding circle around the globe with many a loop and detour. Then a track like a question mark around the Atlantic with the dot at South Georgia. The story of *Curlew*'s remarkable century has encompassed not just her own wanderings but much of the period of South Georgia's exploitation, too. In 1898 Antarctic whaling had yet to begin and there were no whaling station buildings to mar its otherwise pristine shores. We would have loved to see it then. During the next sixty-six years the whales were almost wiped out. And in 1898 it was thought that the fur seals were extinct. Now we are surrounded by more than 2 million. So there is much to be positive about and good reason to hope that South Georgia will represent a rare environmental success story.

Above all else we wish that the name of South Georgia will forever represent an icy paradise, a place where nature is still mostly robust and the way of life of millions of birds, penguins, and seals goes on almost unaltered by the peripheral presence of humans. A clean, pure spring of icy water in our collective consciousness, a soothing, refreshing balm amid the upheavals wrought upon the earth. A precious place to cherish.

INDEX

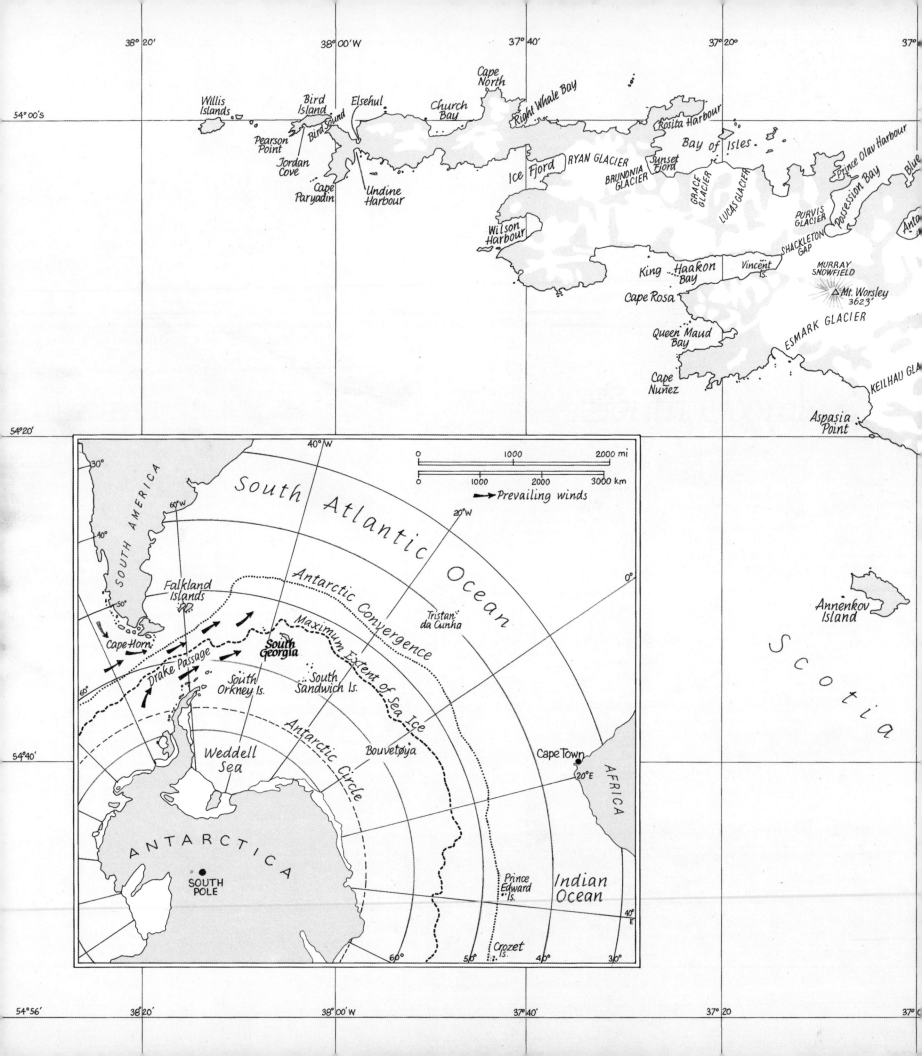

54°00'S

38°20'   38°00'W   37°40'   37°20'   37°

Willis
Islands

Bird
Island

Elsehul

Church
Bay

Cape
North

Right Whale Bay

Rosita Harbour

Bay of Isles

Prince Olav Harbour

Blue

Pearson
Point

Bird Sound

Jordan
Cove

Cape
Paryadin

Undine
Harbour

Ice Fjord

RYAN GLACIER

BRUNONIA
GLACIER

Sunset
Fjord

GRACE
GLACIER

LUCAS GLACIER

Possession Bay

PURVIS
GLACIER

SHACKLETON
GAP

Anta

Wilson
Harbour

King   Haakon
        Bay

Vincent
Is.

MURRAY
SNOWFIELD

△ Mt. Worsley
3623'

Cape Rosa

Queen Maud
Bay

ESMARK GLACIER

KEILHAU GLA

Cape
Nuñez

Aspasia
Point

54°20'

40°W

0   1000   2000 mi

0   1000   2000   3000 km

→ Prevailing winds

30°

SOUTH AMERICA

60°W

South   Atlantic   Ocean

40°

50°

Falkland
Islands

Antarctic Convergence

20°W

Maximum Extent of Sea Ice

Tristan
da Cunha

0°

Annenkov
Island

S C O T I A

Cape Horn

Drake Passage

South
Georgia

South
Sandwich Is.

60°

South
Orkney Is.

Bouvetøya

Cape Town

20°E

AFRICA

Weddell
Sea

Antarctic Circle

54°40'

ANTARCTICA

SOUTH
POLE

Prince
Edward
Is.

Indian
Ocean

40°
E

60°   50°   40°   30°

Crozet
Is.

54°56'

38°20'   38°00'W   37°40'   37°20'